from the
Father's Heart

Hope & Possibilities

DAILY DEVOTIONAL

*Tailored for Life's Seasons -
Emotionally & Spiritually*

MARIA KEAR

From the Father's Heart (Book 4)
*Hope & Possibilities - Daily Devotional
Tailored for Life's Seasons —
Emotionally and Spiritually.*

**From the
Father's Heart
series**

*Rest & Reflection
Growth & Healing
Joy & Adventure
Hope & Possibilities*

Copyright © 2025 by Maria Kear
All rights reserved, including the right of
reproduction in whole or in part in any form.

First Edition August 2025

STM Press
   978-1-966240-06-8 (paperback)
   978-1-966240-07-5 (ebook)

*All scripture references are from the New
Living Translation unless otherwise noted.*

*All word definitions were taken from the
Strong's Online Concordance unless
otherwise noted.*

Designed by Suzanne Parrott
Cover Image created using Midjourney

Acknowledgements

I want to thank my 5 family – Jeff, Matthew, Katherine and Abigail (I'm the 5th) for always cheering me on when I have crazy ideas like writing my own books. Even if they think I'm weird, they still love me.

I want to thank Debra Rothrock and Angie Davidson for their eyes on the text when they had a moment to make sure my grammar and punctuation were in line.

I want to thank Suzanne Fyhrie Parrott for being my publishing partner and the one who made all the details come together so my voice could be heard in the earth.

Dedication

This book is dedicated to the current and future Jesus lovers who will never tire of reading God's Words or of hearing Him speak. To the ones who love and seek out adventure with Holy Spirit as guide and partner. To the ones who are not satisfied with only what this world offers, but long for news from their place of origin – Heaven. And to those brave enough to hug their Bibles to their chests with wide smiles and tear-stained faces. You have found your people!

Author's Note

The first book I learned to read was the King James Version of the Holy Bible. I was five years old when I picked up the book and just started reading. My mom told me that no one taught me to read, but that I just started reading one day.

When I asked her how that was possible, she replied that from the moment I came home from the hospital to live with her and my grandparents Wheeler in Meggett, SC, my granddaddy Wheeler read to me, making sure I could see each page and picture as he read. We believe that his gift of reading to me from day one prepared my brain to be an early and life-long lover of books, especially the Bible.

Thank you, Granddaddy Wheeler.

Day 274

You're all I Want!

Isaiah 62:6-65:25 / Philippians 2:19-3:3 / Psalm 73 / Proverbs 24:13-14

Our lives are filled with so many distractions. Did you know that even a devotional time can be a distraction? What do I mean by that? I spend time reading the Bible every day, and I talk to God, asking Him what He wants to show me through His Word. But I feel I don't sit quietly listening often enough. I would love to make more time for just sitting with Him like one would with a friend. There may be conversations back and forth, and there may be times of quietly smiling at one another.

How do I know God wants this time with us? Because I've experienced it, and every time I've taken the time to sit with Him and have a conversation without all the distractions, He always shows me the most beautiful and amazing things. I've heard words in foreign languages that I had to look up. I've seen pictures that I've drawn or painted, writing down notes to ask for more meaning. I've heard songs, and I've heard Him tell me He loves me.

Without these times, our study time would be unbalanced. There are three verses from my reading today that stood out and caused me to begin thinking this way. The three verses are Psalm 73:25, 26 and 28. Here they are in The Passion Translation.

"Whom have I in Heaven but you? You're all I want! No one on earth means as much to me as you. Lord, so many times I fail; I fall into disgrace. But when I trust in you, I have a strong and glorious presence protecting and anointing me. Forever you're all I need. But

I'll keep coming closer and closer to you, Lord Yahweh, for your name is good to me. I'll keep telling the world of your awesome works, my faithful and glorious God!"

As I read through those verses, I realized they will make a great prayer the next time I sit quietly with the Lord. Sometimes we are at a loss for words when sitting in the presence of royalty, our King. However, we must also remember that this King is our Father, and He loves us beyond words. Have you ever considered asking God what is on His heart as you spend time together? He will always have an answer.

Sometimes we don't ask what's on His heart because we come into prayer with our requests. There is nothing wrong with sharing our heart and our requests with God, but we ought also to listen for Him to speak because He has amazing insight and wisdom, words of love and affirmation, and many other beautiful things to tell us that will make drastic shifts in our thinking and in our daily routine.

I invite you to try it. Make an appointment to sit quietly with the Lord. Leave your phone in another room; I promise you won't miss much while you're separated from it. Try to remove all distractions.

Practicing deep, diaphragmatic breathing will cause your mind to slow down and your ears to perk up. Breathe in slowly for 8 counts, and release for 8 counts. Do that until you notice your mind shifting into an undistracted mode. Then listen.

You're going to hear amazing things! And you'll soon wonder why you didn't spend time with your Father in this way sooner. May God bless your time together and may you hear life-changing words of love and affirmation.

Day 275

No Looking in the Rearview Mirror

Isaiah 66:1-24 / Philippians 3:4-21 / Psalm 74:1-23 / Proverbs 24:15-16

Have any of you ever tried to drive down the road while looking only at the rearview mirror? It sounds dangerous, doesn't it. One of the first things we're taught when we take a driver's education course is to keep our eyes on the road. How might this same principle apply to other parts of our lives?

Paul had lots of reasons to be proud of his past and all the accomplishments he had attained. He was well-educated, came from a good family, and was zealous in his faith. Imagine if Paul, and if we, tried to live his life while only looking at the things he had done and not the things God was still calling him toward.

For one thing, Paul had mercilessly persecuted and murdered followers of The Way. Perhaps we also have some terrible things in our past. Once those things are covered under the blood of Christ and are forgiven, we must no longer focus on what we've done but rather on where we're headed.

Philippians 3 has two verse portions that are interesting to consider. Verse 13b reads,

> "... I focus on this one thing: Forgetting the past
> and looking forward to what lies ahead."

And verse 16 reads,

> "But we must hold on to the progress we have already made."

We must focus our eyes on the road ahead of us. Yes, there are things in our past that we needed forgiveness for, but we are being told to remember our progress and build from there. It's right and good to remember our successes because it is our Lord Jesus Christ who enabled us to accomplish all those good things!

Not only that, when we remember all the good things God has done in and through us, our faith increases, and we're set up to do even greater things in partnership with His Spirit. Our successes not only cause us to feel good about the way we've lived but they also allow us the privilege of the assurance that Jesus Christ is receiving glory from our lives.

When I'm looking forward to what lies ahead, I may not have a complete vision of what the future holds, but as I fall more in love with my Savior, I become more confident that He will lead me into greater and more exciting adventures. When I look back over all the things He's led me through, I remember He is faithful. I remember He is good, and I remember He will not leave me.

Armed with this faith, based on His faithfulness in our lives, we're prepared to conquer anything He leads us to. And we know if He leads us to it, He will walk with us through it. Another aspect of holding on to the progress we've already made is not allowing ourselves to minimize what we have done with His help. We are a team with Father, Jesus, and Holy Spirit; a team that cannot fail because He is on our side.

So, put the pedal to the metal, let the wind blow in your hair, open your mouth wide in laughter, and keep following Him on this adventure. He will never disappoint us! And imagine the amazing stories we'll have to share.

Day 276

Settle Your Disagreements

Jeremiah 1:1-2:30 / Philippians 4:1-23
Psalm 75:1-10 / Proverbs 24:17-20

If we read it too quickly, we can miss a minor issue from Philippians 4:2-3. It appears as if two women who have worked hard along with Paul to spread the Good News, have a breach in their relationship. We don't know what happened, and Paul doesn't spend much time on the topic. He simply tells them to settle the disagreement with the help of one who Paul refers to as his "true companion".

At least Paul didn't tell them to "get over it", or to "grow up" and leave them to themselves to figure it out. He did name a mediator to help them. Sometimes we're able to resolve a relational hiccup, and sometimes we need help.

Divisions, arguments, disagreements, anger, separation in relationships – none of these is fun, but they must be addressed. We as followers of Jesus cannot allow ourselves to remain angry with one another. Yes, there are times when harmful situations won't allow for reconciliation, but, when possible, we must attempt to mend the relationship.

It's best if we can address the other person just the two of us, but if that isn't working, there is a protocol in scripture that is a good guideline for resolving conflict. Matthew 18:15-17 gives a simple outline to follow. As we follow this outline, keep in mind that gossiping or involving others on too wide a scale will muddy these waters and make the situation worse.

Here are those verses:

"If another believer sins against you, go privately and point out the offense. If the other person listens and confesses it, you have won that person back. But if you are unsuccessful, take one or two others with you and go back again, so that everything you say may be confirmed by two or three witnesses. If the person still refuses to listen, take your case to the church. Then if he or she won't accept the church's decision, treat that person as a pagan or a corrupt tax collector."

The hope is that the other person is willing to reconcile with a simple meeting. If not, the one or two more that you take with you should ideally be someone who already knows the situation so that further harm is not done. If someone is genuinely not willing to listen at this point, there is likely something serious going on in her heart and involving leaders in the church is necessary.

When these verses say to take it to the church, I don't believe that means you stand them in front of the gathering and rat them out. There is no reason to shame someone even if they are being unreasonable. Doing so will not cause them to want to change their way of thinking.

Above all, we must treat each other with honor and respect, even if the other person is wrong or is sinning. Why? Because the next dispute may focus on your wrong attitudes or behavior, and you will want to be treated with love and respect in your error.

We are not trying to punish someone just to be mean. The resolution of disputes is meant to bring peace into every heart and to heal whatever has been broken in the natural, spirit, or someone's soul. We must always seek the good of others. We want them to be healed.

So, the next time someone offends you, please think before you act. Remember these verses from Matthew 18. Pray and ask God for wisdom and help, and walk in love. Don't forget that the shoe could be on the other foot.

Day 277

It's Bubbling in My Soul

Jeremiah 2:31-4:18/Colossians 1:1-17/Psalm 76:1-12/ Proverbs 24:21-22

Are any of my readers of a certain age such that you remember this chorus from about the 1970's? "It's bubbling. It's bubbling. It's bubbling in my soul. I'm singing and dancing since Jesus made me whole." I tried to research the song online and couldn't find an author or a date written. Some remember singing this song in the 1950's, so it's been around a while.

If you're wondering what is causing me to think about this bouncy little tune, let's review Colossians 1:11-12.

"May you be filled with joy, always thanking the Father.
He has enabled you to share in the inheritance that
belongs to his people, who live in the light."

How often are we filled with joy? Y'all the world is rough, and there are daily occurrences that threaten to rob us of that joy-filled life. Can we have joy even when circumstances are difficult? I have experienced joy in hardship, so it is possible.

The word "joy" is defined from the Greek as "cheerfulness or gladness." And evidently joy causes us to be thankful. Have you ever met someone who is always smiling, always joyful, and always giving thanks? If someone is always joyful, there must be a reason deeper than their circumstances.

How can we connect into this joy, especially when we are being slammed with difficulty? I'm not saying we can never have a sad, angry, or tearful moment. It is healthy for us to feel our emotions and process them. Maybe the better question is about how we reach the other side to experience joy.

I think the key is just that – the process. So many of us were taught to stifle or ignore our emotions. Or we were told that if we show emotions, we're weak. So, what did we learn to do? We learned to stuff our emotions and keep them inside. But guess what? Stuffing our emotions down causes disease in our bodies. Please don't stuff your emotions.

If you're not comfortable processing emotions alone, please find a safe friend to help you do that. It really is okay to be sad, angry, hurt, lonely, etc. It is healthy to deeply feel the emotion and ask Holy Spirit to help you walk through what you're feeling. He will. God is not afraid of our emotions, even our outbursts!

Once we've processed the feelings of anger, hurt, pain, rejection or whatever is robbing us of peace, there will be joy on the other side. Go for joy! Don't stop at that feeling of helplessness. Push through until you find that settled place in your soul. Your mind and body will thank you. And so will your friends.

Day 278

For the Sake of One

Jeremiah 4:19-6:15 / Colossians 1:18-2:7
Psalm 77:1-20 / Proverbs 24:23-25

It's hard to imagine a city where there is not one person who fears God. Here in the United States, we could easily find at least one person in our friend group who is a sincere lover and follower of Jesus.

Reading Jeremiah 5:1-5 is shocking to those of us who have been raised in the church and raised to follow Christ. I'm not sure when I became aware that there are people who love the kingdom of darkness to the same degree that we love the kingdom of light. Yes, there are those who would rather do evil and follow the plan of the enemy than to follow the light of Christ.

There is one statement of hope in these five verses which proves again how loving God is and how willing He is to forgive and restore humanity.

Verse 1b reads,

"See if you can find even one person who pursues justice.
If you find even one acting with integrity,
I will surely spare Jerusalem."

I appreciate this glimmer of hope as well as the revelation of the extreme heart of love God carries for those He created.

Sadly, in the prophet Jeremiah's time, in the city of Jerusalem, there was not even one person who had integrity. This included the priests who served in the temple. So not only was there corruption and wickedness in the general population, but there was also wickedness in those who were called to serve in God's house. This makes me sick and sad.

It is also hard to believe that there are those in the church today who are pretending to be righteous. Why? There are probably many reasons. It's time we were aware that there are those who seek to infiltrate our righteous communities to pervert the work of Holy Spirit. Y'all, it's time we asked for and operated in discernment. It's time we opened our eyes, awakened our hearts and minds, and acted inside as well as outside the house of God.

While we don't want to believe that evil exists, it does. Once we're aware it exists, we have a responsibility to act. What can we do? We can pray and intercede for our families, friends, communities of faith, our cities, states, and nations. And if we're praying, we can be listening to Holy Spirit. He has strategies for us to implement.

Perhaps He will ask us to drive to a location to pray. Or maybe there is a person or a group of people He wants us to impact in some way. He may compel us to give our finances to those in need. He may ask us to take someone out for coffee, looking for opportunities to strengthen them in their faith.

I can't tell you what action plan He'll lay out before you, but I can exhort you to do what He says. Each of us can pray and act. One thing we must not do is stay silent and still in the face of evil around us. What if we obey His leading and someone is delivered from evil. If the Lord acts on behalf of one, we must do the same.

Day 279

The Foolishness of the Cross

Jeremiah 6:16-8:7 / Colossians 2:8-23
Psalm 78:1-31 / Proverbs 24:26

After our scripture reading yesterday, and the call to discernment and awareness of evil that would try to infiltrate our lives, there is another equally dangerous attempt to pull us away from the truth. Some might argue that both distractions are from the same source. One is defined as from the kingdom of darkness and the other is referred to as "arguments of human logic."

Whatever your core belief about the source of these two evils – whether both enemy strategies, or one human and one enemy – we must be aware and guard against anything that would distract us away from the truth of God's Kingdom. This is another call for skilled discernment. We cannot afford to be lazy in our walk with Christ. Colossians 2:8 is jam-packed with valuable insight.

"Beware that no one distracts you or intimidates you in their attempt to lead you away from Christ's fullness by pretending to be full of wisdom when they're filled with endless arguments of human logic. For they operate with humanistic and clouded judgments based on the mindset of this world system, and not the anointed truths of the Anointed One."

If you are not aware of the term "humanism", I feel this is a good place to define that term to bring some clarity for what we must guard against. "Humanism", according to the dictionary is defined as "a doctrine, attitude, or way of life centered on human interests or values." At first, this may not seem like a bad thing. However, when we dive deeper, we will see the dangers of following our human logic and doctrines.

Scripture tells us to renew our minds. Romans 12:2 from The Passion Translation,

"Stop imitating the ideals and opinions of the culture around you
but be inwardly transformed by the Holy Spirit through
a total reformation of how you think."

There is a difference between our human logic and the wisdom of God. This is not to minimize the beauty of the human mind that God gave us, but if He is telling us to reform our thinking, there is something we need to align with that comes from His Spirit that is not innate to our existence. We need God's wisdom!

1 Corinthians 1:25,

"This foolish plan of God is wiser than
the wisest of human plans, and God's weakness is
stronger than the greatest of human strength."

The "foolish plan" referred to here was described in the preceding verses of the chapter. But this is a great display of God's wisdom.

To some, the cross of Christ is foolish, as is the preaching of the Gospel. It seems foolish because Christ chose the weakness of being born into a human body to give His life for our sins. This is where we get into trouble if we try to understand God's plan from a human perspective! Yet, the decisions the Father made to send His beautiful Son to us brought salvation and freedom. This is the Good News of the Gospel.

Romans 1:16,

> "For I am not ashamed of this
> Good News about Christ.
> It is the power of God at work,
> saving everyone who believes..."

This "foolish" sacrifice of God brought us life when nothing we could do in our humanity could bring anything good. This "foolishness" is true power. It is the power to save us, free us, deliver us from the power of evil. I'll choose God's wisdom above human wisdom every time, and that is where we gain discernment.

Day 280

Thoughts of Home

Jeremiah 8:8-9:26 / Colossians 3:1-17
Psalm 78:32-55 / Proverbs 24:27

Have you been on the earth long enough to figure out this is not our home? I understand that our first thoughts when someone says they are going home are of their state, city, or actual house. Even when my youngest moved to Alabama, I still called Tennessee her home. I wasn't willing to admit she might be choosing a new place to call home that was separate from her momma.

When Colossians 3:1b TPT tells us to "yearn for all that is above, for that's where Christ sits enthroned at the place of all power, honor, and authority!" Our first thoughts are to be reminded of who we are in Christ. And that should be our first thoughts because then we realize that in Him we also have all power, honor and authority to extend His Kingdom into the earth.

If that's where Christ is seated, and He is ours and we are His, our next thoughts could naturally be that wherever He is, that is our home. You've heard people say to a loved one that wherever they are is home. Meaning that it's not a physical location that is necessarily the home; it's the people we're connected to.

And that is so true! While I currently reside in Knoxville, TN on Fort Sumter Road, I also consider Charleston, SC to be my home because that's where I was born. When my thoughts go back even further, I realize that even before I was born into the earth, I was conceived in the heart of God.

"And in love He chose us before He laid the foundation of the universe! Because of His great love, He ordained us, so that we would be seen as holy in His eyes with an unstained innocence."
— Ephesians 1:4, TPT

So, when I use the logical, left side of my brain, I must conclude that I was born in Heaven and therefore, that is my true home. Yes, I'm being serious, but also a little tongue-in-cheek. If you find yourself longing for Heaven, and to see the face of Jesus, your first Love, now you know why. Your DNA is calling out for your place of origin.

When my daddy left earth in October 2016, and then my momma in April 2023, my first response upon hearing was deep laughter from the Spirit. Why? Because I knew they had gone home. Yes, after that I sobbed because I will miss them so much.

This may sound strange, but they don't feel that far away to me. Maybe it's because the realms are very close in proximity. Maybe it's because I'm aware that they are standing in the great cloud of witnesses cheering me on. Maybe it's because my last breath here will be my first awakening there and I will see them in the blink of an eye.

While this topic could make some sad, it gives me great hope, massive joy and a peek into the rejoicing to come! We're here for such a short time, and while here we are blessed through God's Spirit so that we can be a blessing to the earth and the people here. And when our life's mission has been accomplished, we will head back home for a great celebration!

Day 281

Get Even, or Forgive?

Jeremiah 10:1-11:23 / Colossians 3:18-4:18
Psalm 78:56-72 Proverbs 24:28-29

The words of Proverbs 24:29 are direct and clear.

"And don't say,
'Now I can pay them back for
what they've done to me!
I'll get even with them!'"

Y'all, I can't count how many times I've wanted to get even with someone who hurt me. And it didn't need to be getting even by my own hand. It was fine if "fate" got them, or God got them. I just wanted them to pay for the pain they had caused. Then I realized, not only was I refusing to forgive, but I was also knocking at the door of bitterness.

Verse 29 above tells us not to say these words! No payback. No getting even. No wishing harm upon another person for any reason. You may be thinking, "But they are so evil!" I understand. Honestly, they will naturally reap what they've sown because of the laws of nature and because of God's spiritual laws of sowing and reaping.

But we must not even secretly hope for that reaping to come to pass, because that is the same as wishing evil upon someone. So, what do we do? First, we forgive the offense. You might pray something like this.

24

This is step one:

"Lord, I choose as an act of my will to forgive <name>
for <tell what they did to you or another>."

Then when you're ready, please pray for "crop failure." Do they deserve that? Probably not. But did you deserve anything good? Probably not. However, God loved us when we were "dead sinners." Therefore, we must love one another.

"But God is so rich in mercy, and He loved us so much, that even though we were dead because of our sins, He gave us life when He raised Christ from the dead. (It is only by God's grace that you have been saved!)" — Ephesians 2:4

No human deserves any more or less than another. Jesus Christ died for all people. He didn't look down and say, "Oh wait! That one looks better than those others, so let's save just that one." No. He died for all, regardless of origin, background, past, sin, or family history. We are all in the same boat.

Our original boat could be titled "Death through Sin." And we were all sitting in that boat, happily rowing ourselves into oblivion. Then He looked down and saw the trouble we were in. He saw where we were headed – straight into the land of "Separation from God" – and He had mercy on us.

He brought to every single one of us a new boat with the name "Rescued by His Blood" and He invited every person to say, "Yes" and to climb into this rescue boat. Some will receive this rescue, and some will reject it. Regardless of that choice, it is our privilege to walk in forgiveness toward every person who has harmed us.

I hope you hear the heart of the Father here. We are all in need of forgiveness. There are times when we need someone to pray that the crops we've sown will not grow to be harvested. After that, please connect with Holy Spirit and pray blessings upon the one who harmed you.

If someone offends you, please forgive them. Please pray for crop failure for what they've done, and please pray blessings over them. Pray their eyes are opened. Pray they receive His love and forgiveness. You would want someone to do the same for you.

Day 282

Until We See His Face

Jeremiah 12:1-14:10 / 1 Thessalonians 1:1-2:8
Psalm 79:1-13 / Proverbs 24:30-34

Two days ago, we talked about our real home and the sweet anticipation of returning to Heaven one day. Today, I want to talk about what makes that homecoming so sweet. The sweetness is not in the sights we'll see, or in the people we will be reunited with (even though that will be amazing!). The best part of going home will be in finally getting to see our Savior face to face.

If you're like me, you've often wondered what that day will be like. What will He look like in person? What will His voice sound like? What will we do together? The good news is we'll have the rest of eternity to explore all of that with Him and with those who have gone before us.

1 Thessalonians 1:10a reads,

> "And they speak of how you are looking forward
> to the coming of God's Son from Heaven –
> Jesus, whom God raised from the dead."

How could anyone speak of these desires unless they had heard them spoken? That tells us that the Thessalonian church must have had a culture of longing for the return of Jesus. They must have talked about Him often. And their talk probably made others long to see Him as well.

How often do we think about or talk about getting to see Jesus?

Sure, we hear Him speak to us through His Word, through others, or within our own hearts. So, we have a measure of knowing Him now. But there is still so much mystery because the veil between earth and the Heavenly realm still exists.

One day that veil will be removed completely. There will be nothing that separates us from seeing His face and hearing His voice. We will laugh with Him, run with Him, and worship Him in person! Oh, my goodness! I could almost come out of my skin just thinking about how wonderful that will be.

And as much as we might imagine what all of that will be like, I have a strong feeling we have only a sliver of understanding. And that feeling is based on several scriptures, one of which I'll include here.

> "Dear friends, we are already God's children, but
> He has not yet shown us what we
> will be like when Christ appears. But we do know
> that we will be like Him,
> for we will see Him as He really is."
> —1 John 3:2

We don't know what we will be like, but we will be like Him. As His children, we will be like our Father. I can't wait! This reminds me of another verse from Acts 17:28.

> "For in Him we live and move and exist.
> As some of your own poets have said,
> 'We are His offspring.'"

Day 283

Plead with, Encourage, and Urge

Jeremiah 14:11-16:15 / 1 Thessalonians 2:9-3:13
Psalm 80 / Proverbs 25:1-5

We must be constantly working to bring the best out in others; to remind them of who God created them to be and of their value to Him. I guess I shouldn't be surprised that so many are unsure of the stamp of God on their lives since we have an enemy that is continually fighting against us. If we were ever fully aware of our worth in God's Kingdom, we would be unstoppable. Our adversary can't have that happen!

1 Thessalonians 2:11-12 talks about the bulk of the work a Christian leader faces daily. Here is what these two verses state:

"You know that we treated each of you as a father treats his own children. We pleaded with you, encouraged you, and urged you to live your lives in a way that God would consider worthy. For he called you to share in his Kingdom and glory."

There have been times I wished I was confident in who God created me to be in the earth. And there have been times I wished others were also confident in this same way. I grow weary at times of reminding myself that I am a daughter of the King, and there are also times I wonder if others are listening when I remind them of their identity in Christ.

Recently, during a house church gathering, one lady pointed to me saying that I have encouraged her not to identify herself with the labels of others, but only with the labels God gives her. Someone is listening! That was so encouraging to me; my words are being heard, and they are producing life in someone else's heart. It's a blessing to see the fruit of our hard work. Not everyone gets the opportunity to see the growth God brings.

Three words from the verse above are fascinating. Those words are "pleaded", "encouraged", and "urged." Let's look at each of these words because they do not sound like "light" actions being described. In the King James Version of the Bible, "pleaded" is the word "exhorted", "encouraged" is the word "comforted" and "urged" is the word "charged."

"Exhorted" means "to call near, invite, call for, comfort, desire, entreat, pray."

"Comforted" means "to relate near, console, encourage calm or comfort."

"Charged" means "to be a witness, testify, give evidence, bear record, give testimony – to affirm that one has seen or heard or experienced something, or that he knows it because taught by divine revelation or inspiration."

That sounds like a lot of hard work on the part of our leaders! Some believe we can speak into a person's life once and they should understand what they must do, but the truth is we must repeatedly exhort, comfort and charge our brothers and sisters in Christ because they are being repeatedly fed a contrary message. Some can encourage themselves; some need lots of help from others, and some need help from time to time.

The level of encouragement we need depends on many factors such as how long we've been a follower of Jesus, what maturity we've gained by using God's word, the circumstances we're facing, and many other factors. Even the strongest of believers has seasons that are so difficult that they need help from God and other believers. I don't think we can assume that even our leaders do not need encouragement; they do. After all, we are all human, clay vessels and we "leak", requiring a refilling.

We must first recognize that we need encouragement. Then we are free to approach God's throne of grace to get the help we need. We can approach that throne alone, or we can invite another to do that with us. Sometimes inviting another to come along with us will also encourage her! Don't try to live your life in a lonely vacuum; reach out for help from others. They may point you to God, take you to God, or carry you there if needed!

Day 284

Run to the One Who Knows You Best

Jeremiah 16:16-18:23 / 1 Thessalonians 4:1-5:3
Psalm 81 / Proverbs 25:6-8

Raise your hand if you've ever felt alone or misunderstood. While I can't see your hands, I have a feeling that all my readers have their hands up. I know mine is up. I believe we are misunderstood partly because others are focused on their own needs and situations. There is nothing wrong with that!

If we are misunderstood, we must begin with an attempt to communicate our hearts and our needs. Even when we do that, we will not always be received or understood, but at least we will have tried. And, sadly, not everyone will understand us. Not everyone has the time or the capacity to really hear what we are trying to convey, except One who is perfect and knows us well because He made us.

If we're feeling that no one "gets" us, no one will listen, or our needs are not being met, we must scoot up a chair and share our hearts with God. He always listens and He understands completely. Even those who love us most, our families, do not always understand. When that happens, we have two choices; get upset and shut down or go to God to sort through our feelings.

The following two verses remind us that when we're feeling misunderstood, not heard, overlooked, or ignored, we have a place to go for strength and renewal. As I typed that, I had the thought that perhaps we should go to God first, then try to explain our hearts to those we love. It's probably a good plan to go to the Manufacturer/

Creator first, get that understanding and help we need then share with those we love.

Jeremiah 17:7-8,

"But blessed are those who trust in the Lord and have made the Lord their hope and confidence. They are like trees planted along a riverbank, with roots that reach deep into the water. Such trees are not bothered by the heat or worried by long months of drought. Their leaves stay green, and they never stop producing fruit."

The word "blessed" is a rich one, so I want to look at that one further, along with the words "hope" and "confidence." As for the rest of the verse, consider yourself a tree, or put your name in place where the tree is spoken of.

The word "blessed" has as one of its first meanings "to kneel." When I think of someone kneeling with their head bowed, I think about an honor or blessing being bestowed upon them.

There is also an indication of "abundance" or "greatness" with the blessing. How do we get that blessing and abundance? We are blessed when we trust in the Lord, and when we make Him our hope and confidence. When I trust Him, I am safe and secure, as well as confident and bold. If He is my hope, He is my refuge or safe place, and He also makes me confident.

Here is the definition for "hope" which also includes the word "confidence": "trust, confidence, refuge, act of confiding, object of confidence, security." I love that hope can be described as the "act of confiding." That means we can freely share with the Lord what is on our hearts. We can tell Him what we might not feel safe telling anyone else. He cares, will not judge us, and will bring His rest and peace to us.

So, even if no one understands us, and even if we're feeling insecure about what we believe, He is saying that we must remember that He is the One who identifies us! Others may think they know or understand us. Others may even try to label us according to who they believe we are, but if this labeling doesn't line up with what God has said about us, we are completely within our rights to reject those labels. And I have done just that; rejected the labels.

How have others labeled you? Are they seeing you correctly? If they are, keep those friends nearby because they are a treasure and asset in your life. If you have been spoken of in a way other than God's design, feel free to toss those words and put a little space between you and the one who does not properly see you.

Don't be rude or throw the friendship away, just be wary of them until you either have time to develop the friendship to a point of understanding or to discover that this person may not need to be in your close friendship circle.

We can't be besties with everyone! However, let's do be besties with our Lord and Savior Jesus Christ. He is the One who confirms and affirms us because He knows how and why He created us.

37

Day 285

Be Careful Little Ears What You Hear

Jeremiah 19-21 / 1 Thessalonians 5:4-28 / Psalm 82 / Proverbs 25:9-10

Have you ever felt you were the last to know something? Or that everyone else understood the topic, except you? Some call that "being in the dark" or "being asleep at the wheel", neither of which is a very comforting place to be found.

As people of God, we do not have to live in darkness, confusion, or a lack of understanding. We have Holy Spirit who helps us with discernment and wisdom in every situation.

1 Thessalonians 5:4-8 gives us clear instructions on who we are as people of the light. This is what it says,

"But you aren't in the dark about these things, dear brothers and sisters, and you won't be surprised when the day of the Lord comes like a thief. For you are all children of the light and of the day; we don't belong to darkness and night. So be on your guard, not asleep like the others. Stay alert and be clearheaded. Night is the time when people sleep, and drinkers get drunk. But let us who live in the light be clearheaded, protected by the armor of faith and love, and wearing as our helmet the confidence of our salvation."

It's important that we know who we are and who we are not as followers of Christ. We are surrounded by information overload every day from media, books, and other people's opinions. But there is only one opinion that matters and that is God's. As we're wading through everything that comes our way, we must be able to separate truth from lies. Those who are in the light have an advantage because we have Holy Spirit telling us clearly what truth is.

We aren't in the dark about the Day of the Lord's return (the statement on "these things" referred to in verse 4). We won't be surprised when that day comes. We are children of light and of the day. We don't belong to darkness or night. These are the facts of who we are because we are in Christ. I think you should read those again and read them aloud using "I am" statements. For example: "I am not in the dark about the Day of the Lord's return."

If you somehow feel you are in the dark, I encourage you to ask God to show you what you need to know. He will be faithful to do that. And as you continue to declare the truth, your heart and understanding will be opened by Holy Spirit to receive what you need. Because we are children of light, there are some things expected of us.

We are to be on guard. We are not to be asleep like the others. We are to stay alert and clearheaded. We are to be protected by the armor of faith and love, wearing a helmet that is our confidence of salvation. If we are alert and confident of our salvation, we have everything we need for the Day of the Lord's return.

We don't know the exact day He is coming, but we know we are ready. So many worry about knowing the day, even trying to predict that day. Scripture tells us that no one knows the day, except the Father (Mark 13:32). If only the Father knows, it must be that we should not be concerned about that.

I believe we must remain alert to our relationship with the Father through our Lord Jesus Christ. If we place that relationship first, then endeavor to share what we know with others, we and them will be prepared and will miss nothing. We do not need to know everything to be considered ready.

Are you awake and ready? If Jesus Christ returned today, would you be prepared to meet Him? Would your loved one or friend be ready? These are the questions that matter. That's why we must not be distracted by worthless things such as living the way the world does.

Stay alert, be clearheaded. Filter what you listen to, watch, and speak about because these are the things that will either further strengthen you in your faith or tear you down and cause confusion.

I realize this is a huge task because the messages around us are loud and many. But you can do it! "Be careful little eyes what you see; be careful little ears what you hear. For the Father up above is looking down in love, so be careful little ears what you hear."

Day 286

Our Response to Suffering

Jeremiah 22:1-23:20 / 2 Thessalonians 1 / Psalm 83 / Proverbs 25:11-14

Many people throughout history have sought to make a name for themselves. It's human nature to want to live well and leave a legacy. All of us want to be remembered for the good things we've done, and we hope that the mistakes we've made will be forgiven and forgotten.

Have you ever considered that as Jesus followers we have another name to make great? And how can a human house the Sovereign Lord and do His name justice? Those are some big shoes to fill!

2 Thessalonians 1:12 is written as a prayer for the people of God in the city of Thessalonica. Because of this prayer, we have hope that we will be able to honor the name of Jesus Christ through our clay vessels. Here is what that verse states:

> "We pray this so that the name of our Lord Jesus
> may be glorified in you, and you in Him, according to
> the grace of our God and the Lord Jesus Christ."

The church in this city lived under heavy persecution yet they stood strong in their faith. Verse 11 tells how Paul, Silas and Timothy were praying for the church. Their prayers included that their every desire for goodness would be brought to fruition, and that every good deed would be prompted by faith.

The prayers were not to remove the persecution, but that goodness and faith would reign during suffering. It is during times of trial that Christ is most glorified in us. It is easy to stand strong when we're experiencing only blessing; the true test comes when we are being tested with lack or hardship.

What does it mean that the name of Christ is "glorified" in us? I think it's time for a word study! The word "glorify" means "to praise; to magnify and honor in worship; to ascribe honor to, in thought or words."

It's interesting that the definition mentions our thoughts. Nothing comes out of our mouths unless we have first thought about what we're going to say. Some give little thought before speaking and some give much thought. Our words may seem to be giving praise, but if our hearts are set in another direction, our words will be hollow.

How does one give glory to God in troubled times? We can't simply pretend we are not suffering when we speak. It's in those times of difficulty that we must build our praise on the goodness of God and not on the circumstances we are facing. God is good no matter what is happening. Evil and trials come to everyone, but that does not change God's character.

Verse 11 mentions a desire for goodness. What does "goodness" mean in this verse? The definition of the Greek word used for goodness is "uprightness of heart and life, or kindness."

Think about it. The people of God were suffering persecution, yet they maintained a right heart and were kind to those around them. Many would be angry and try to either defend themselves or attack those who were attacking them. Maybe the believers in Jesus knew that their kind response when facing persecution would allow those who did not believe in Jesus to listen to the message of the Good News.

Paul, Silas, and Timothy spoke of being thankful for the brothers and sisters in this city because their faith was growing, and their love was increasing even while they were being unfairly harassed. I'm sure these Jesus followers were an example to many.

What about you and me? How do we respond when we face personal injustice? Do we respond with anger, or disbelief that we would be treated this way? I have been guilty of both, and much more. The Lord is still working in my heart to quickly forgive those who are unjust toward me. I pray you allow Him to do the same for you.

Day 287

Getting Stronger as You Age

Jeremiah 23:21-25:38 / 2 Thessalonians 2 / Psalm 84 / Proverbs 25:15

Have you ever walked through a dark season that seemed to sap all strength and hope from your soul? I would say you have because all of us face such seasons. I wish it weren't so, but it is part of living on planet earth to experience suffering of various kinds. Some suffering is light and manageable, and some suffering has the potential to completely wreck one's soul. I pray the latter never happens to you.

I have been through several seasons that threatened to wreck my soul and my faith, but God has faithfully been with me through them all. There was a season in early 2018 that caused me to consider walking away from fellowship with other Jesus followers. We had been deeply wounded by those we had been with for many years, and I remember telling my husband that if this was how the body of Christ treated one another, I was done.

Thankfully neither my husband nor my Savior would allow me to walk away. And deep in my heart I knew better. I simply needed time to forgive and heal. I've been walking that healing journey since then and I have grown by leaps and bounds because I did not give up. I did not allow what I now see as an attempt of the enemy to derail me, to take hold. God is faithful.

As I read Psalm 84 today, I was blessed by these words that I've read many times. I was reminded why I stay on this path that God drew me to, placed me on, and continues to give me grace to walk. I'm here because of Jesus Christ. I began because of Him; I stay because of Him, and I will finish because of Him. I'm so thankful that He is the One who keeps me!

Psalm 84:5-7,

"How enriched are they who find their strength in the Lord; within their hearts are the highways of holiness! Even when their paths wind through the dark valley of tears, they dig deep to find a pleasant pool where others find only pain. He gives to them a brook of blessing filled from the rain of an outpouring. They grow stronger and stronger with every step forward, and the God of all gods will appear before them in Zion."

When we're feeling anger, depression, sadness, hopelessness, or any other emotion that would attempt to derail us from God's path, we must remember that we find our strength in the Lord. We find strength not just for today, but to continue all of life's journey until we see God face to face in His holy city, our true eternal home.

That highway of holiness is referred to in this way in the New Living Translation:

"Who have set their minds on a pilgrimage to Jerusalem."

We have left our home, Heaven, and are now traveling through earth as a pilgrimage toward our home once again. When our hearts are fixed on and thinking about Heaven, our journey is filled with God's grace and spiritual provision.

The path will be rocky and difficult at times, but we will grow stronger with every step forward. Most would experience going from strength to weakness as they traveled, but that is not so with God as our source of life, hope and strength. With God our strength increases.

This thought process reminds me of Caleb in the Old Testament. Caleb was 85 years old before he was given the land God promised him in the Promised Land. At the age of 85 Caleb defeated the giants that were in his land, and he settled down to live the rest of his life. Scripture doesn't tell us how long Caleb lived but based on the account in Joshua 15:14 Caleb was strong and powerful even at 85 years old! I want to be like Caleb!

Based on the verses in Psalm 84 we have the potential to be stronger and stronger as our days go by. I'll take it! What about you? Would you like to become stronger instead of weaker as you live the rest of your days? Evidently it is a possibility. I bet it has to do with digging deep to find a pleasant pool when others are finding only pain. That sounds like a Kingdom perspective to me.

In wrapping up, we can find Kingdom perspective by reading the Bible, praying and being in relationship with Jesus Christ, and by keeping ourselves in community with other Jesus followers. Yes, I have concluded that it's best to remain connected with His body, and God has blessed me with an amazing community of Jesus lovers!

Doing all of this is no easy task, but it is doable. So, the next time life feels hard, dig deep, and find the Lord's pleasant pool so that you can gain new strength.

Day 288

Dealing with Lazy Bones

Jeremiah 26-27 / 2 Thessalonians 3 / Psalm 85 / Proverbs 25:16

How does it make you feel when someone is always asking you for help or handouts but not reciprocating? I enjoy being generous but when I notice that the other person is only receiving and not willing to give, I tend to back off on my giving a bit. Of course, it's important to hear Holy Spirit because we don't give only so we will receive. More important than expecting our relationships to be balanced in this area is that we hear God and obey Him.

However, scripture does talk about that if someone will not work, they should not eat. I understand that sounds harsh and I can't imagine allowing someone to literally starve to death because they aren't working. I think the point being made is once that belly starts to grumble, the lazy person should be motivated to work!

In our reading today I took note of the context of the verses in 2 Thessalonians 3.

> "Keep away from every believer who is idle and
> disruptive and does not live according to
> the teaching you received from us."
> — 2 Thessalonians 3:6

The Passion Translation says it this way:

> "Stay away from believers who are unruly and
> who stray from all that we have taught you."

"Unruly" is defined in the notes as "undisciplined, lazy, or not in battle order or not in your duty station." There is an implication that there were some believers in the city who simply refused to work for a living. Paul had set an example of working to make a living while he also fulfilled his call to ministry. Paul appears to be saying it is improper for the church to support those who refuse to work. Personal responsibility is a big deal.

Living in community requires that all have a part to play and an area in which they are encouraged and expected to give. Community works because all are giving what they have for the sake of others. In this way, no one is left wanting or needy. Perhaps if we still lived this way, the broken welfare system would not be needed. I will not open that can of worms here.

How do we balance grace and mercy with truth in this area? I believe we give people every opportunity to get back on their feet and change, but when it becomes apparent that one is not willing to bear his or her own burden, it's time for a discussion. If exhortation works, it's great. If not, it's time for the lessons of life to speak for themselves.

At least when able-bodied adults are involved. If the elderly, disabled, or children are involved, let's step up as the body of Christ and help those who are truly in need. Part of the problem is there are not many who are truly in need apart from the orphans and widows referred to in scripture.

Let me clarify that in abusive situations that abused person is an orphan in my book and is worthy of help getting back on her or his feet. We do not leave someone in an abusive situation, nor do we counsel them to stay. We help them get out and support them as a community.

If the church of Jesus Christ were operating according to scripture, I do believe our world systems, along with our households, would look more stable and be stronger. There is something to be said for multi-generational communities living together and sharing strengths as well as needs.

The next time you see someone in need, pray first about how to help instead of beginning with judgment. Time will tell what type of person you have in front of you, and no gift given with a sincere heart is ever wasted in God's eyes.

Day 289

His Overflowing Grace-Fountain

Jeremiah 28-29 / 1 Timothy 1 / Psalm 86 / Proverbs 25:17

Have you ever had the view of God that He was angry, waiting for you to make a mistake so He could punish you? I suppose if you were raised in a strict or abusive household that you might be inclined to believe that your Heavenly Father is also strict and abusive, but nothing could be further from the truth. God is loving and kind toward those who are His. However, I wouldn't want to be on His enemy list!

Psalm 86:5-7 in TPT is a sweet reminder that tells what a relationship with our good Father looks like.

"Lord, you are so good to me, so kind in every way and ready to forgive, for your grace-fountain keeps overflowing, drenching all your devoted lovers who pray to you. God, won't you pay attention to this urgent cry? Lord, bend down to listen to my prayer. Whenever trouble strikes, I will keep crying out to you, for I know your help is on the way."

These verses describe our Lord as good, kind, and ready to forgive. I believe He wants us to see Him as all these things, and that our prayers and repentance release goodness, kindness, and forgiveness to us. I also believe that He pours a measure of all three of these out on us daily, but that God also longs to open that grace-fountain and drench us.

The Lord is not stingy; He is a God of abundance. He has gifts and favor to give to us that far surpass our expectations. The trouble is sometimes our expectations are too small because we don't understand how large our God is. I mean we're talking about the God who created all the universe by simply speaking words. If He can create a universe through His speech, I'm positive He can bless us to overflowing.

I love that the Psalmist is confident that help is on the way when he prays. Are you confident that God will hear and answer when you pray? Sometimes I am confident and sometimes my faith wavers. But I know He is always listening because I belong to Him. I may miss a few things when listening to my children and grandchildren, but God doesn't miss anything.

Not only does He hear every word we speak, but He can also "hear" the longing in our hearts. He hears our hopes, dreams, fears and disappointments and they are all important to Him. He doesn't forget a single detail regarding the things that are important to us.

Which brings me to remember the verses in Matthew 6:25-34 where Jesus taught the crowds not to worry. I will post only verse 25 for you here; please feel free to read the rest from The Passion Translation.

"This is why I tell you to never be worried about your life, for all that you need will be provided, such as food, water, clothing—everything your body needs. Isn't there more to your life than a meal? Isn't your body more than clothing?"

When we believe that all we need will be provided, our prayers change from those where we beg without hope, to knowing God will answer. When we are confident God hears and is answering, our lives are filled with peace. I pray that as you read today, God's Spirit brings the confidence you need to pray, trusting God is already at work on your behalf. He loves you so much!

57

Day 290

I am God's Favorite

Jeremiah 30:1-31:26 / 1 Timothy 2 / Psalm 87 / Proverbs 25:18-19

If you think women are treated without respect or dignity at times, that's true. However, Jesus showed an example of the heart of the Father toward women in that He had several women who were part of the company of His disciples. They were shown the same care and concern as the male disciples. Jesus even stopped to speak with a Samaritan woman at a well, something that Jewish men usually did not do.

The bottom line is that Jesus didn't look at whether one was male or female before deciding on that person's value in His Kingdom. Galatians 3:28-29 TPT further shows us God's view of all people.

"And we no longer see each other in our former state—Jew or non-Jew, rich or poor, male or female—because we're all one through our union with Jesus Christ. And if you belong to Christ, then you are now Abraham's "child" and a true heir of all his blessings because of the promise God made to Abraham!"

Only through our relationship with Jesus Christ are we made the same in God's eyes. We are now Kingdom people and heirs of all God has. It seems that Jesus is the great equalizer. And if He looks at all of us as equal, we should also view each other with equality.

I believe part of this equality is because we are now spirit beings, so we are viewed first from that perspective instead of from external perspectives. What if we treated one another according to a Heavenly perspective instead of based on how much money we make, or what job we have, or how much education we have acquired, or our gender, or our past, etc.?

I also don't believe we should evaluate one another based on spiritual gifting or position in the church, or even by the number of years we've been following Jesus Christ. This perspective is informed by the parable about the vineyard workers from Matthew 20:1-16. Throughout the day the owner hired workers, paying them the same wage whether they were hired early in the day or late in the day.

The ones hired early in the day were upset that those hired later in the day received the same wages, but the owner asked them why they were upset when they were paid the agreed upon price. It is the same with those in God's Kingdom. Our wages are eternal life, and we are all on equal footing regardless of when we received God's gift of salvation.

The one who came later is of no less value than the one who came earlier and vice versa. We have all received the same gift for the same price that was paid – the life of the one unique Son of God. We should be thankful that many others have had their sins forgiven and eternal life given to them.

The Christian life is not a competition to see who "wins". We all win! Remember that we are winning by no means of our own worth, but by means of the value of how Jesus Christ paid for us on the cross. Even when we win, Jesus Christ deserves the thanks and praise for our victory.

The next time you "side glance" another Jesus follower, please check your heart. He or she is of equal value to God. Despite what some say, God does not have favorites. We are all His favorites!

Day 291

Destroy the Enemy's Plans

Jeremiah 31:27-32:44 / 1 Timothy 3 / Psalm 88 / Proverbs 25:20-22

Have you ever thought about what you would do if faced with an enemy? I have. Unfortunately, I do have those who despise me. Let me define the word despise before I go on with what I have to say. The word "despise" from Merriam Webster's dictionary means "to look down on with disrespect or aversion, despise the weak or to regard as negligible, worthless, or distasteful."

I wish there were not those who saw me this way. Maybe you can relate. It's hard knowing there are those out there who have ill feelings toward you. I have worked hard to forgive those who fall into this category. Sometimes I've had to forgive them several times.

One day the Lord asked me a question. He said, "If those who have treated you this way came to your door needing food, water or shelter, would you give it to them?" That was a hard question, because I sincerely do not want to spend any time in the presence of those who despise me. But if anyone who feels this way toward me came to my door in need, I would help them.

If they were a danger to my life, I would not necessarily invite them in, but I would send them away with food and water, or whatever I had to spare. I could not send someone away hungry or thirsty in good conscience. Why? Because no matter how someone has treated me, they are beloved image bearers of God, and I know it's His heart that we care for one another.

Proverbs 25:21-22 TPT tells us,

"Is your enemy hungry? Buy him lunch.
Win him over with your kindness.
Your surprising generosity
will awaken his conscience,
and God will reward you with favor."

In awakening our enemy's conscience, we are impacting his heart and exposing his shame. Perhaps that will cause repentance to come into his heart, and he will be freed from the consequences of his actions and attitudes.

If repentance comes to our enemy, we will have done him a great service of love. I would be happy for that to happen for those who see themselves as my enemy. Some believe I should wish evil for them in return. One who has forgiven cannot do that. One who has forgiven has a heart to pray for blessing and favor on those who are mistreating her.

It's taken me a long time to get to this point, so I understand if you are not quite there. I do, however, want to encourage you to ask God how He can help you walk through forgiving, loving, and praying for those who have hurt you. Remember, you are doing these things to bring freedom to your own heart. The other person may never know what you have accomplished.

Forgiveness is not for the other person; it is for you. If you want a heart right before God, and if you want the ability to move into blessing in your life and relationships, I implore you to forgive those who have hurt you. You will never regret having done so.

Then, if you have an opportunity, do something to bless that "enemy" and see if God would also change her heart. Who knows, maybe you can be the one who helps restore a clean heart to one who previously hated you. Not only should that make you feel good about what you've done, but that should also make you feel joyful that you have destroyed the enemy's plan in your life.

I *love* destroying the enemy's plans.

Day 292

God the Covenant Keeper

Jeremiah 33-34 / 1 Timothy 4 / Psalm 89:1-13 / Proverbs 25:23-24

Covenant is a word we don't use much these days. Perhaps the people of God are familiar with the word and what it means biblically. There is also a legal meaning behind the word covenant. Marriage is an example of a covenant. Let's define this word from the Merriam Webster dictionary then let's talk about biblical covenant.

> "Covenant" is defined as "a usually formal, solemn, and binding agreement. A written agreement or promise usually under seal between two or more parties, especially for the performance of some action. The common-law action to recover damages for breach of such a contract."

> "Covenant" as a verb is defined this way: "to promise by a covenant: pledge. To enter into a covenant: contract." This is what we do when we marry someone or agree to business arrangements, etc.

In a covenant there are always at least two parties. One would not make a covenant with herself or himself – usually. But wait! There's more that I'll explain in a minute.

In the Old Testament when a covenant was established one of the customs was to cut an animal down the middle, and place the two halves some distance apart, allowing the two parties to walk in a figure 8 pattern between the two halves.

It's hard to know all the possible penalties for breaking such a covenant, but I'm sure that as serious as the covenant making was, you would not want to be caught breaking the agreement. I'd say some scary consequences awaited the one who broke covenant. In Jeremiah 34:19, the leaders of Judah and Jerusalem made covenants in the way described above, but they had broken their covenant.

As a result of these men breaking the covenant they had made, they were being taken into captivity by Babylon, and some of them were going to die. It appears as if one should soberly enter these type covenants with God. Perhaps they did not count the cost of what would happen should they not uphold their end of the bargain.

In Jeremiah 33:23-26, God is declaring that He does not break the covenants that He establishes. He does not break His side of the bargain, ever.

The wording is strong when He tells Jeremiah this:

"If I have not made my covenant with day and night and established the laws of Heaven and earth, then I will reject the descendants of Jacob and David my servant and will not choose one of his sons to rule over the descendants of Abraham, Isaac, and Jacob. For I will restore their fortunes and have compassion on them."

If God has promised that He will do something, He will never go back on that promise. We are fickle, God is not. When God made His covenant with Abraham in Genesis 15, He did not allow Abraham to walk between the two halves of the animal. God walked for both parties.

God took both sides of the covenant. God made an unbreakable covenant because He made the covenant with Himself. I know of nowhere else in history where one made a covenant with himself – at least not a legal, binding covenant.

Perhaps you have made pledges and promises to yourself, but that is different. We are always going to be imperfect in our ability to keep our promises; God is never imperfect. If God has said something to you, He will accomplish what He said.

So, when you've said, "Yes" to His beautiful salvation, it is He who will perform the work in you. As you keep saying, "Yes" to Him, He will cause you to look more like Him. You may fail, but He will not!

I encourage you today to allow God to be the covenant initiator as well as the covenant keeper in your life. He knows your weaknesses. He sees your best efforts and loves you, but we can never outdo God when it comes to covenant.

Day 293

Wellspring or Muddied Spring?

Jeremiah 35-36 / 1 Timothy 5 / Psalm 89:14-37 / Proverbs 25:25-27

All of us make mistakes and commit sin. And all of us do good deeds and make wise choices. I've noticed something lately and that is some people have gotten "soft" regarding what the Bible tells us is sin. However, I do not believe we should beat people over the head for their sins and mistakes; conviction is God's job.

What is our role when we see a brother or sister overtaken by sin? Galatians 6:1 in the New Living Translation is helpful. It tells us this:

"Dear brothers and sisters, if another believer is overcome by some sin, you who are godly should gently and humbly help that person back onto the right path. And be careful not to fall into the same temptation yourself."

If we see someone we love heading down a path that will trap them by sin and consequences, we should speak up. But we must do so in humility, realizing we could be the ones caught by deception and sin. After all, no one is immune to sin. If you see the sin and you're angry or judgmental, it would be better to pray and ask God to give you a right heart before or if you address the situation.

Not every situation is ours to address either. I am personally more likely to speak to someone in my immediate family if I notice something harming them. If I see a friend who is harming herself, I will pray and ask God what my response needs to be. Then I must follow God's leading on my action.

As for strangers, it's not likely I would intervene unless I was a witness to immediate danger or harm of another. For example, I've often overheard strangers speaking with anger or contempt to their children and while that hurts my heart, I will not get involved. If I saw someone being physically harmed, I would have to do something. I would probably make an emergency call to avoid physical danger for myself.

Then there is the matter of the world watching us as followers of Christ. If we are actively involved in sin, we are marring the beautiful name of Jesus. I realize we are not always aware that we're sinning. But I also have on many occasions felt the sting of Holy Spirit conviction as I've headed in a direction in my thoughts or actions that would not honor the Lord.

Proverbs 25:26 struck me as I read it today because I'm aware that the world is especially watching those of us who claim to belong to Christ. This is what that verse states:

> "Like a muddied spring or a polluted well
> are the righteous who give way to the wicked."

I don't know about you, but I don't want to be seen or known as a "muddied spring" or a "polluted well". That sounds dirty, nasty, and unfavorable at the least! Pondering this topic reminds me of what Proverbs 4:23 TPT tells us about our hearts.

> "So above all, guard the affections of your heart, for they affect all that you are. Pay attention to the welfare of your innermost being, for from there flows the wellspring of life."

I much prefer having a wellspring coming out of my heart to having a muddied spring coming out. How do we cultivate a wellspring? We must desire a clean, clear, and refreshing flow both for ourselves and others. We must guard our hearts. From what must we guard ourselves? We must pay attention to the things that grab our love and affection.

If we're concerned about what others think of us, we may find ourselves doing things we would otherwise not do. If we believe we are without the things we need, we might find ourselves stealing. If we feel trapped in a situation, we may begin to tell lies. There are many scenarios that could potentially trap us. I pray you have someone in your life who loves you enough to warn you when they see danger ahead.

And I pray you listen when that one who loves you comes with the warning. Even if they bungle the delivery, they are usually speaking up in fear and trembling because they love you too much to watch you being robbed by the devil. The devil would love to see you continue in sin so he can rob you blind. May you be set free from all deception and sin today!

Day 294

Is Money Evil?

Jeremiah 37-38 / 1 Timothy 6 / Psalm 89:38-52 / Proverbs 25:28

There is something that irritates me; well, there are several things that irritate me, but today we'll talk about only one. I'm sure you're relieved! One of my biggest pet peeves is when people misquote or misrepresent scripture. It doesn't take much time or effort to look up a verse you're trying to remember so you quote it properly. When scripture is misquoted, the meaning is usually totally changed.

I've heard people say, and I've seen it written, that money is evil, or money is the root of all evil. I cringe every time someone says or writes that. Money is an inanimate object and cannot by nature be evil. Objects are not evil, people are. The same could be said for guns, but I don't want to open that can of worms today!

This is what the often referred to verse, in 1 Timothy 6:10, actually says.

"For the love of money is a root of all kinds of evil.
Some people, eager for money, have wandered
from the faith and pierced themselves with many griefs."

The love of money is "a" root of "all kinds" of evil. "A" means one of several and "all kinds" means there is also more than one. As said above, money is not "the" root of all evil. I will dare to say that the devil is the root of all evil. And his influence in the hearts of men and women spreads that evil across the earth.

There are other sayings I've heard that people attribute to the

Bible and that is equally disturbing to my sense of truth. Here's one, for example, "The Lord helps those who help themselves." Nope, not in there. And does that mean if I don't help myself, He'll ignore me and let me suffer? I've experienced the opposite. God has stepped in many times when I'm drowning and unable to help myself.

Let's look back at our verse about money being the root of all kinds of evil. What kinds of evil might this verse be referring to? Greed, control over others, thievery, unkindness toward those in need - just to name a few. Let's focus on what our attitude toward money ought to be.

We put our hope in God, not in wealth. We are to do good, and that includes giving of our resources – time, treasure, and talent. We are to be rich in good deeds instead of seeking to be rich monetarily. Not that there is anything wrong with being rich, especially if one uses that wealth to further God's Kingdom. And finally, we are to be generous and willing to share.

None of that sounds like a Scrooge or a miserly person. God expects us to live with the perspective of abundance and generosity in every area. We cannot be small thinkers, or selfish or stingy. If you notice yourself being that way, it's time to find a place to give what you have, whether that is your time, your resources, or your heart.

The Father is our example of a loving, unselfish giver in that He gave His one unique Son to us to reconcile us back to Himself. If the Father would give His beloved Son, what could we consider giving? I know of one other father in scripture who was asked to give up his son. God asked Abraham to sacrifice Isaac. Of course, God provided an alternate sacrifice and Isaac lived to fulfill the promise of filling the earth with Abraham's legacy.

God does not physically ask us to give up our children, but He certainly asks us to give them to Him spiritually. That means we are not to worry about them. Truthfully, we are not to worry about anything we need. If God is asking you to give, you can be assured He will provide both what you need and enough extra to satisfy the needs of others around you.

I encourage you to ask God where you can be a blessing today. Then, quickly make it happen!

Day 295

Protect or Attack

Jeremiah 39-41 / 2 Timothy 1 / Psalm 90-91 / Proverbs 26:1-2

Are you one of those who feels compelled to guard, watch over or look after others? You may be the type that can't stand when injustice, injury or harm comes to someone you love, or even to a stranger. The thought of another human being suffering is too much for my tender heart. Even if that person is evil and deserves punishment, my heart hopes they will repent. I have a soft spot when it comes to others being harmed, compelling me to want to guard them.

Let's look at the example of those on sports teams whose job it is to guard the opposing team from scoring. Some enjoy the guarding position, which is a defensive position, and some enjoy the offensive or "attacking" roles. In the Gospel, I believe we must operate in both positions. There are times we must protect and there are times we must attack.

2 Timothy 1:12-14 instructs us on some things that must be guarded. Let's look at those verses in the New Living Translation.

"That is why I am suffering here in prison. But I am not ashamed of it, for I know the one in whom I trust, and I am sure that he is able to guard what I have entrusted to him until the day of his return. Hold on to the pattern of wholesome teaching you learned from me—a pattern shaped by the faith and love that you have in Christ Jesus. Through the power of the Holy Spirit who lives within us, carefully guard the precious truth that has been entrusted to you."

There are two parties guarding something in these three verses. First, the Lord is guarding what we have entrusted to Him. And second, we are to guard the precious truth that has been entrusted to us through Holy Spirit's power. What exactly is each party guarding? Let's look!

We are trusting Jesus Christ to guard everything about our lives both naturally and eternally. We trust him with our physical lives; He knows the number of days He has given us. We trust Him with our eternal salvation. We must also trust Him with our reputation, our resources, those we love and anything else we can think of that might cause us to worry. If you are worrying about it, it's because you have not entrusted that thing to Him!

With all things we hold dear firmly in God's care, what are we to guard? The precious truth. Some today believe truth is relative to the situation, or that not all truth applies to every person. We must remember that absolute truth is a person that does not change or waver. In that light, there is a truth we must guard and that is the truth of the Gospel of Jesus Christ.

There is only one way to be reconciled to the Father. There is only one way to receive forgiveness of sin. There is only one way to be fully and purely known and loved. Some find a type of truth in the world, but that truth will crumble when the earth is finally destroyed to make way for a new Heaven and earth. Only the truth that is found in Jesus Christ will withstand when the judgment of God is complete. Because of that, we must be found hidden in Christ Jesus.

Staying hidden in Christ is our only hope of escaping judgment and destruction. However, let's remember also that our relationship is not solely about an escape plan; we are hidden in Christ for the sake of receiving His protection, care and love. Everything we have trusted Him with is safe and secure and nothing that happens either on this earth or in Heaven will ever be removed from His mighty hand.

Day 296

Let's Flourish like Palm Trees

Jeremiah 42:1-44:23 / 2 Timothy 2:1-21 / Psalm 92-93 / Proverbs 26:3-5

I don't know where you are regarding your season of life. You may be young, middle-aged, or older. You may be single, newly married, married with children, or a grandparent (one of the most amazing roles one can fulfill!).

One thing is sure; we all have a certain number of years to live on planet earth. As a matter of fact, God already knows the number of our days. I personally take comfort knowing that He has lovingly planned my days.

As I approach the "fall" season of my life – what I see as the third quarter of my years – I am beginning to consider how I want to spend the rest of my time. I plan to live a long life; I'm asking God for 120 years like Caleb's number of years on earth. My dad asked for the same number of years, but God invited him to join Him in Heaven at the age of 78. Whatever God has planned for me, I trust Him.

We all want to live our years well. We want to honor God, love people, and leave a strong legacy for our children, grandchildren, family, and friends God has placed in our lives. We want to be re-membered for having loved God and loved people. We are not quit-ters or those who do things half-heartedly. We are tenacious, strong, loving and kind.

If you were to ponder your legacy and how you want to spend your remaining years, whether many or few, how would you want to be remembered? We must first plan, then we must faithfully do small things every day that align with that plan. Planning without action will not leave the legacy we desire.

I love the verses in Psalm 92:12-15. Here are those verses in The Passion Translation, (TPT.)

"Yes! Look how you've made all your devoted lovers to flourish like palm trees, each one growing in victory, standing with strength! You've transplanted them into your Heavenly courtyard, where they are thriving before you, for in your presence they will still overflow and be anointed. Even in their old age they will stay fresh, bearing luscious fruit and abiding faithfully. Listen to them! With pleasure they still proclaim: 'You're so good! You're my beautiful strength! You've never made a mistake with me.'"

We could stop there because that describes so well what a beautiful legacy would look like. Who does not want to flourish like a palm tree? Or to grow in victory and strength? Spiritually, we've been transplanted from an earthly existence and perspective to a Heavenly one (although our physical body is still planted on earth!). We are thriving, we overflow, and we are anointed. Even in old age, we can be fresh and bear fruit. What amazing promises!

Let's get more understanding of a few words from the verses in Psalm 92. I want to look at the word "flourish" and its meaning. I want to look at the word "strength," and finally, I want to look at the words "abiding faithfully." These are some amazing words to explore.

"Flourish" means "to bud, sprout, send out shoots and blossom." That describes every stage of growth. I especially like that we will send out shoots because that speaks of giving what we have to others. And "blossom" is indicative of bearing fruit. Bearing fruit is a strong sign of a healthy and growing person.

The word "strength" (as stated in TPT) refers to "growing like a cedar of Lebanon" (NLT). The picture here is that a cedar tree grows strong because of the tenacity of its root system. Cedar trees are tall and widespread, also denoting stability and strength.

"Abiding faithfully" in TPT is stated as
"staying fresh and green," in the NLT, and as
"fat" in the KJV.

And no, I'm not calling any of us fat! This meaning is spoken of as "substantive, vigorous, and stalwart" in the Strong's Concordance.

My prayer is that all of us will find ourselves living according to this beautiful legacy until we leave earth. We can maintain a loving, beautiful heart and we can trust God that our physical bodies will allow us to fulfill His will until we are also invited to join Him in Heaven.

Day 297

Scripture is the Breath of God

Jeremiah 44:24-47:7 / 2 Timothy 2:22-3:17 / Psalm 94 / Proverbs 26:6-8

The very first book I learned to read was the Bible. I credit my Granddaddy Wheeler with my learning to read so early and well. Because my daddy was in the Navy, my momma and I lived with my grandparents while she was pregnant and until I was about 9 months old. My mom told me that from the moment I came home from the hospital, my granddaddy would sit me in my baby carrier and read to me, even showing me the words and pictures in the books.

My mom said that no one taught me to read – I wasn't yet in school – but that one day I just started reading. And as I said above, the first thing I read was the King James Version of the Bible. Thank you, Granddaddy, for reading to me!

It's a well-known fact that children who are read to become early and better readers. They are better spellers, and I would say they have an excellent command of the English language. Read to your babies and grandbabies!

Perhaps my love of the Bible as God's Word came from those early memories of reading. I don't know what books Granddaddy read to me. Maybe he read the Bible. I'm sure he read classic children's books.

By the time I was 5, I was reading, and I was ready for salvation. Seeds of the Gospel had been planted in my heart. I'm sure God will tell me when I see Him how all that happened. I'm just grateful it did! Because I have loved God's Word for so many years, the verses in 2 Timothy 3:16-17 grabbed my attention today.

"All Scripture is inspired by God and is useful to teach us what is true and to make us realize what is wrong in our lives. It corrects us when we are wrong and teaches us to do what is right. God uses it to prepare and equip his people to do every good work."

Here are those same verses in The Passion Translation.

"God has transmitted his very substance into every Scripture, for it is God-breathed. It will empower you by its instruction and correction, giving you the strength to take the right direction and lead you deeper into the path of godliness. Then you will be God's servant, fully mature and perfectly prepared to fulfill any assignment God gives you."

Unfortunately, we are living in a time in history when many do not believe the Bible is infallible and divinely inspired. Some argue that the words, intent, and meanings have been changed and that we are missing parts of scripture that ought to be included. Whether that is true or not, I know that God guards His own Word and that what we have available has living power within the pages.

Perhaps the reason some make the statements is that they are hesitant to be accountable to the truth contained in scripture. I love The Passion Translation where it says: "God has transmitted his very substance into every Scripture, for it is God-breathed." That tells me all I need to know.

Even if parts are missing or have been misinterpreted, we have enough available to live the godly life God desires.

Remember 1 Corinthians 13:9-12 in TPT, which states:

"Our present knowledge and our prophecies are but partial, but when love's perfection arrives, the partial will fade away. When I was a child, I spoke about childish matters, for I saw things like a child and reasoned like a child. But the day came when I matured, and I set aside my childish ways. For now, we see but a faint reflection of riddles and mysteries as though reflected in a mirror, but one day we will see face-to-face. My understanding is incomplete now, but one day I will understand everything, just as everything about me has been fully understood."

Even God's Words tell us we see and know in part, so none of us can expect to have a full revelation or knowledge on this side of eternity. We must trust God with what we have, believing that He is able to make up the difference by His Holy Spirit and our relationship with Him. We are missing nothing when we have the Spirit of God living inside us!

The Bible, and the Holy Spirit, are correcting, teaching, preparing, and equipping us for everything God has planned for us to accomplish while we are on earth. Read His Word, listen to His voice and take action to accomplish the things you're hearing Him say. I promise you have enough available to you to please and honor God with your life!

Day 298

Decrees over the Nations

Jeremiah 48:1-49:22 / 2 Timothy 4 / Psalm 95-96 / Proverbs 26:9-12

Do you ever wonder what path to follow in life? There are so many options, opinions, choices, and decisions to make that it can be overwhelming. I'm usually a decisive person but there are times when I'm not sure what I should do. Today I'm having one of those dilemmas and I know that only my Heavenly Father has the answer.

Sometimes your family member or friend can't tell you what to do because God wants to tell you Himself. When God brings you an answer it will never violate His written Word. You will find principles in His Word to guide every decision you make.

I've heard some say that the answer to their question is not in the Bible. Your answer may not appear specifically, but there will always be a precedent set that will guide you toward truth. Be sure you're reading it regularly so Holy Spirit can bring the words to your mind.

The Father will sometimes allow another to answer, and He will sometimes wait for you to sit with Him and wait quietly to hear what He has to say. At other times, you may experience answers from both places to help give wisdom to your situation. Today I have questions about the nations. What is my role and responsibility toward nations and people who live there?

In reading Psalm 96 I found the beginnings of some answers, but I'm realizing I'll need to continue to sit with the Father so He can unfold His heart on the matter. Here are the five verses I found to help me so far.

Verse 3: "Declare His glory among the nations, His marvelous deeds among all peoples."

Verse 5: "For all the gods of the nations are idols, but the LORD made the Heavens."

Verse 7: "Ascribe to the LORD, all you families of nations, ascribe to the LORD glory and strength."

Verse 9: "Worship the LORD in the splendor of His holiness; tremble before Him, all the earth."

Verse 10: "Say among the nations, 'The LORD reigns.' The world is firmly established, it cannot be moved; He will judge the peoples with equity."

As I was reading the above verses, I thought of one more that was pulled from the depths of my heart by Holy Spirit. Psalm 33:12 in The Passion Translation states:

> "Blessed and prosperous is that nation
> who has God as their Lord! They will be the people
> He has chosen for His own."

As I read these verses, I remembered that not every nation has God as their Lord. My nation once had God as their Lord, but we have strayed away from our firm faith these past many years. Thankfully, I am seeing a return to the Lord by a remnant of believers, among whom I am.

I'm thankful that my heart has remained steadfast and fervent for the Lord in this season of life. It's not an easy season to remain steadfast and many are falling away from their faith and from fellowship with other believers.

As I'm praying for the nations and the people who live within them, I now have some decrees I can make over the 195 nations of the earth. I can decree over them His glory and marvelous deeds, imploring them to see and remember all He has done. I can decree that the nations who are serving idols will have their eyes opened to the truth. I can decree that the nations will ascribe to the Lord the glory and strength He deserves.

I can decree to the nations to worship the Lord and tremble before Him – not in fear, but in reverence and awe. I can decree to the nations that the Lord reigns and He will judge all people equally. And I can decree blessings over the nations whose God is the Lord.

As I said, I'm sure I'll find other things to decree as I read, communicate, and study. But this is a great beginning in answering my question. I didn't expect to find the answer today, but I made myself available to worship and communicate with God and He saw the questions on my heart, so He answered! That's amazing to me!

Day 299

The Sounds of the Spirit

Jeremiah 49:23-50:46 / Titus 1/ Psalm 97-98 / Proverbs 26:13-16

The realm of the Spirit is not a quiet place. I can think of one place in scripture where it says there was silence in Heaven. Revelation 8:1 in The Passion Translation reads,

> "When the Lamb broke open the seventh seal,
> Heaven fell silent for about half an hour."

What followed was terrifying. Maybe that's why all Heaven was silent; they knew what was about to happen. But for now, while we're in the season prior to the terrible day of the Lord, there are sounds all around us that we only hear with Spirit ears.

Psalm 98:7-9 in TPT tells us this,

> "Let the ocean's waves join in the chorus with their roaring praise until everyone everywhere shouts out in unison, 'Glory to the Lord!' Let the rivers and streams clap with applause as the mountains rise in a standing ovation to join the mighty choir of exaltation. Look! Here he comes! The Lord and judge of all the earth! He's coming to make things right and to do it fair and square. And everyone will see that he does all things well!"

I don't know about you, but when I read those verses, I hear all the sounds mentioned. I don't hear with my natural ears, but my spiritual ears hear, and I understand a small portion of the beauty of these sounds. Imagine oceans roaring in praise, or rivers and streams clapping as mountains rise in a standing ovation.

Luke 19:40 tells us in TPT that "stones would break forth with praises!" That causes me to wonder what else in creation is making a sound of worship and praise to the One who created all these things. Each created thing understands the Creator because the essence of the Creator is within each of those things. His power, love, eternal nature, and many other aspects of His character are present in the molecules of nature causing it to be alive and "noisy".

When God spoke, the power of His word not only created all we see (and don't see) but it also embedded in all things the energy of God. If you're a science lover, you know that all of creation is made up of atomic and subatomic particles. The particles we can't see are atoms and are made up of protons, neutrons, and electrons. These are not even the smallest particles. There are quantum particles that are even smaller. But they all have one thing in common: energy.

There would be no energy in the world apart from God. Our bodies run on energy. If we had no energy, our bodies would not operate. When scientists discovered this energy, some did not realize the source of all the energy in the universe was the Lord who created it all.

Hebrews 1:3 mid-verse in TPT says,

> "He holds the universe together
> and expands it by the mighty power
> of His spoken word."

That power is the energy man has harnessed for our use.

When we get to Heaven, I believe our minds will be blown away to discover all the things we haven't known or seen. As vast and powerful as God is, I have a feeling we've only scratched the surface of the things He created for us to discover. And make no mistake, man does not create new things, he uncovers and discovers the hidden mysteries God has placed for him to find.

There are mysteries everywhere, and the sound of the praises of creation is just one of those beautiful mysteries. So, the next time you're enjoying nature's beauty, remember that all the things you see are singing, clapping, and worshiping God. Be careful not to allow nature to praise more or better than you do!

Day 300

Instructions for Men and Women

Jeremiah 51:1-53 / Titus 2/ Psalm 99 / Proverbs 26:17

The Bible is our instruction manual for life. Some say the Word of God is not relevant or that it is fallible since it was written by men. I say it is the divinely inspired Word of God and has the power for salvation contained in its pages; not because of the words themselves, but because of the One who is the Word both written and revealed.

If we are unsure how we ought to live or how we should behave in a certain situation, studying God's word will inform us. We must be willing to read, study, meditate upon and act on God's word for it to "work" in our lives. God's word is living and powerful. (Hebrews 4:12)

There are some instructions in Titus 2 that will apply to everyone. The text begins with instructions for the older men, then some instructions for both the older and younger women. The entire chapter is beneficial, so I encourage you to read all of it in either the New Living Translation, (NLT) or The Passion Translation (TPT).

Let's begin with instructions for the men since that's where Titus 2 begins. Verse two tells us to "teach the older men to be temperate, worthy of respect, self-controlled, and sound in faith, in love, and in endurance." Let's look at each of these instructions to see what the men are being instructed to follow.

What does it mean to be "temperate?" It means "abstaining from wine, either entirely or at least from its immoderate use." What does it mean to be "worthy of respect?" "To be venerated for character, honest."

How does one operate as "self-controlled?" "To be of a sound mind, sane, in one's senses. Curbing one's desires and impulses."

How does one become sound in faith, love, and endurance? To "become sound" means "to be in health, i.e. be well (in body); figuratively, to be uncorrupt (true in doctrine)."

"Faith" is defined as "conviction of truth."

"Love" is defined as "affection, goodwill, and kindness."

"Endurance" is defined as "the characteristic of a man who is not swerved from his deliberate purpose and his loyalty to faith and piety by even the greatest trials and sufferings."

Now, let's get some instructions for the older women. Beginning in verse three the older women are told to "be reverent, not slanderers, not to be addicted to much wine, and to teach what is good." If the older women are living this way, they can urge the younger women in how they are to live.

What does it mean to be reverent? Reverence speaks of "being holy or set apart to and for God." When a woman is reverent, she does not operate according to the mandates of the earth, but according to the mandates of Heaven as found in scripture.

What is slander and how may we avoid it? Slander refers to false accusations. The Strong's Concordance says this: "May be said to act the part of the devil or to side with him." That is very sobering. I would never want to act like or side with the devil.

Not being addicted to much wine is self-explanatory. However, I will say this; this is not saying we should not drink wine, but we must not be drunk. If we feel free in our hearts to drink wine, we still have a few parameters. One is that we should be moderate in our consumption. The second is we must be aware of those around us so that our behavior is not offensive. If we are around someone who is struggling or has struggled with alcohol addiction, it is loving of us to abstain in her or his presence.

How are we as women to teach what is good? First, we must know and study good things such as God's Word. Then as we take in the truth contained and we put these things into practice, we are free and mandated to teach what we've learned and practiced to others. In my opinion, God's truth is the "good" that has been spoken.

Finally, what about the younger women? Verses four through five give instructions for the younger women. They are to "love their husbands and children, be self-controlled and pure, be busy at home, be kind, and be subject to their husbands."

To keep this entry at a good length, I will not dive deeper into these final topics but will encourage you to take time to look up this verse in the online Strong's Concordance for yourself.

Day 301

Our Words Can Be Destructive

Jeremiah 51:54-52:34 / Titus 3 / Psalm 100 / Proverbs 26:18-19

Our words matter; what comes out of our mouths not only reveals what is in our hearts, but those words will also build up or destroy those who are listening. I'm sure you would rather be known as a builder instead of a destroyer. Our words will either produce life, health, and peace, or death, disease, and chaos in those we are talking with.

As I read Proverbs 26:18-19 today I was struck by how evil our words can be both for ourselves and for others. I will give you these two verses both in the NLT and in TPT because I believe the sobriety of what you'll read will impact you even more with both versions.

Proverbs 26:18-19 NLT,

> "Just as damaging as a madman
> shooting a deadly weapon
> is someone who lies to a friend and
> then says, 'I was only joking.'"

Proverbs 26:18-19 TPT,

> "The one who is caught lying to his friend,
> who says, 'I didn't mean it, I was only joking,'
> can be compared to a madman
> randomly shooting off deadly weapons."

The scenario depicted here disturbs me both because I despise lying and because the destruction it causes is spoken of very graphically here. First, when someone speaks and then says they were only joking, you can be assured there is at least some measure of truth to their words, or they would not have been spoken.

> "Out of the abundance of the heart,
> the mouth speaks."—Matthew 12:34

When one speaks you can be assured that the words are based on something they believe either consciously or subconsciously. Or the words come because they are speaking of what they've been pondering. We can quickly know what a person believes, along with the health of his or her soul by listening to the words they share.

I especially noticed that the words being spoken here are from a friend. So, this is someone who you know well and who also knows you. This person would know your hurts, trials, joys, etc. That means they should be more careful about what they speak over and to you.

The comparison of "a madman shooting a deadly weapon" (NLT) or "a madman randomly shooting off deadly weapons" (TPT) makes these unthoughtful words especially harmful. If you were speaking with a friend who you loved, you wouldn't grab a weapon and start shooting at her! But that is what we're doing when we don't choose our words wisely.

Think before you speak. Consider who you're with and what that person needs. Consider what Holy Spirit may want to bring that would encourage and build up the one you're talking to. A follower of Jesus Christ cannot be flippant with her words. Once those words have been spoken, the damage can sometimes be irreparable. Yes, repentance and forgiveness can take place but once someone's soul has been wounded, we never know how long that healing may take.

I am not saying you can't poke fun, make jokes, and cause one another to laugh. Laughter is good and fun. But be careful not to allow your words to cause harm to the other person, because even in laughter someone may be hurt. And sadly, they may not tell you they are hurt. They may silently bear the pain without you ever knowing the damage caused.

If someone ever approaches you to let you know that your words hurt them, receive what they are saying with humility and be willing to apologize and ask forgiveness. What hurts them may not hurt you so you may not understand their pain. It doesn't matter whether you understand or not; you must still make things right for the sake of the other person and the relationship. Then, next time you're speaking, you will be more careful with your words.

Day 302

Take the Wood Off the Fire

Lamentations 1-2 / Philemon / Psalm 101 / Proverbs 26:20

Perhaps all of us have been guilty of the sin of gossip, talebearing, slander, spreading rumors or stories, or whatever one might call this behavior. Sometimes the gossip is hidden in the desire to share a "prayer need" with another. Sometimes the story is information that should not be shared with another. Sometimes the information is true, sometimes it is skewed by our own opinion, and sometimes it's an outright lie.

It's a good rule of thumb that unless the person who is the topic of conversation is present and requesting that the information be shared for the sake of their freedom or healing, it should never be shared. Yes, I am boldly saying that. I have unfortunately been the recipient of some who believe it's okay to spread stories, rumors, and lies behind my back to others. And let me tell you, it's hurtful and I've had to forgive people many times.

No matter what the motive for sharing, the listener will find themselves tainted toward the object of gossip. The listener may also develop a poor opinion of the person speaking the gossip, so beware. You may think you're not ruining your own reputation by spreading rumors, but I promise you are.

It's crazy to consider that one person would treat another that way, but it happens all the time. I believe it's time for some Holy Spirit conviction on the matter. You may remember that we've talked about the damage our words can do. This is an example of that. Gossip is when words are being used to tear down and destroy another human being who God loves.

Don't let yourself get caught in this trap! If you want to talk about someone, tell the good parts. Lift that person up. Confirm their good character, generous deeds, and heart. Find something good to say or say nothing at all. As usual, one of today's verses has me considering this subject.

"Without wood a fire goes out;
without a gossip a quarrel dies down."

And because TPT is also a favorite of mine, here is that verse again.

"It takes fuel to have a fire—
a fire dies down when you run out of fuel.
So, quarrels disappear when the gossip ends."
— Proverbs 26:20

That's quite the picture of wood on the fire because one can easily imagine that the more wood is added, the greater the fire. When wood is no longer added, the fire eventually dies down and goes out. Therefore, we must stop adding wood to the fire of gossip.

If you've been guilty of the sin of gossip, go to the one you have injured or poisoned and ask forgiveness. The words cannot be taken back, and they have already caused damage, but you can certainly pray that God will heal and repair the damage that has been done.

He can help you clean up the mess left behind by the harmful words spoken. You'll have to be bold and take the initiative in repairing the situation. First, you'll have to admit you were wrong for the words spoken. It will take humility, and swallowing that pride, and that is not an easy task, but your soul will feel so much better! When we repent and ask forgiveness for sin, our souls feel so much lighter.

"But if we freely admit our sins when his light uncovers them, He will be faithful to forgive us every time. God is just to forgive us our sins because of Christ, and He will continue to cleanse us from all unrighteousness." — 1 John 1:9, TPT

When God says, "Light uncovers" that you have sinned, it is a powerful statement. God uncovers sin in us because He sees the damage sin does to our souls. He knows that sin creates death in us, and He wants us to experience His abundant life. Repent from sin and choose life. Not only will those who you hurt be glad you've changed the way you think, but you also will be happier.

Day 303

The Lord's Great Love

Lamentations 3 / Hebrews 1 / Psalm 102 / Proverbs 26:21-22

Yesterday we talked about the sin of gossip. Today I want to bring comfort to you. Once we've been confronted with our sin, the Lord will always try to bring love and strength to us, so we won't become discouraged about our imperfections. Most are painfully aware of their shortcomings and not always as aware of how loved they are.

Romans 5:8, in TPT reads,

> "But Christ proved God's passionate love for us
> by dying in our place while we were still lost and ungodly!"

God didn't wait for us to figure out we were sinners and separated from Him to provide a way for us to escape from our chains. He saw us in our dirt and with our evil hearts, and He had compassion for us. The Father sent His Son when we could do nothing to free ourselves from bondage.

John 3:16 in TPT says,

> "For here is the way God loved the world—
> He gave his only, unique Son as a gift. So now everyone who
> believes in him will never perish but experience everlasting life."

God loved the world when we were a terrible mess, and we had no idea of how awful we were because of our sin. That's amazing love! I'm still in awe that God doesn't love me because of how wonderful

I am; He loves me because He created me, and I am His. The same is true for you. You cannot be more wonderful and cause Him to love you more – He loves you fully as you are. Let that sink in.

Today I want to highlight Lamentations 3:22-24 in the New International Version.

"Because of the Lord's great love, we are not consumed, for his compassions never fail. They are new every morning; great is your faithfulness. I say to myself, 'The Lord is my portion; therefore, I will wait for him.'"

Even if you have sinned today, made a mistake, or were imperfect, He still loves you! Your sin does not remove His love. Jesus died on the cross to pay for every sin you have, do, and will commit. Forgiveness is always available so that you are free to walk away from that sin. I encourage you to walk away because as you walk, you will find love, healing, and freedom.

All of us are looking for peace: for our hearts not to be burdened down by grief, sorrow, tragedy, and evil. There is only one place to find true peace and that is in being confident you are loved unconditionally by the Father. And you are! Believe it. Receive it. Walk in it.

Because of His love, you will not be consumed, you will not die, you will not be overrun by evil. His compassions never fail. What are His compassions? They are His tender love. Also, in Strong's Concordance, the definition we find for the word "compassions" refers to "the womb and the cherishing of that baby in the womb." That's very powerful love!

What does it mean for you to realize the Father loves you and to say, "He is your portion?" The word "portion" means: "my share, my territory, my possession." In other words. "God is mine. I am His and He is mine." I love that! I've said before to the community of Jesus lovers around me, "You are mine and I am yours." I had not yet considered that the same could be said for Jesus Christ. Beautiful!

May you know, receive, and walk in His great love today, tomorrow, and for the rest of your life. Be blessed!

Day 304

The Strength of His Love

Lamentations 4-5 / Hebrews 2 / Psalm 103 / Proverbs 26:23

There are negative messages around us all day, every day. It is the rare person who is filled with encouragement and strength because of the words of those around them. If you have that encouragement, count yourself amazingly blessed! Especially during the times in which we are living, there is so much negativity in the natural and spiritual realms that one must dig deep to access the strength the Lord brings.

Today's inspiration is taken from Psalm 103:11-12, it tells us this,

"For as high as the Heavens are above the earth, so great is His love for those who fear Him; as far as the east is from the west, so far has He removed our transgressions from us."

"As high as the Heavens are above the earth." This phrase does not refer only to the Heavens we can see. It does not refer only to the place where the sun, moon, and stars reside. The Heavens are the universe that has no end, as well as the dwelling place of God. I believe this phrase is speaking of an infinite quality, especially because God's great love is being compared to the height of the Heavens. God's love cannot be measured.

There is a prayer in Ephesians chapter three that Paul prayed on behalf of the church in Ephesus. Part of that prayer in verse eighteen says this:

"May you have the power to understand,
as all God's people should, how wide, how long,
how high, and how deep His love is."

The love of God covers every area you could possibly consider. From the above description, God's love covers all things. That sounds like encouragement and strength to me. This is an area we must rehearse and believe so we can combat the negativity thrown at us continuously.

What else does the verse tell us? Our loving God has removed our sins from us "as far as the east is from the west." What does that mean? If you've ever traveled across the world or to the other side of the world, you know that you will eventually come right back to where you started if you keep traveling. I have traveled to Cambodia which is about halfway around the world from me in Knoxville, TN.

If I were to have kept traveling, I would have ended up home again. It's as if God is saying, you can keep traveling in these circles from east to west (eventually you will not know whether you are traveling east or west) and you will never find the sins of which I've forgiven you. Our sins get lost in His love and forgiveness.

Micah 7:19 says,

"Once again you will have compassion on us.
You will trample our sins under your feet
and throw them into the depths of the ocean!"

That sounds violent! God hates our sin so much that He will trample them under His feet and throw them into the deep part of the ocean. He is destroying and burying our sin. He hates sin because of what it does to our souls and bodies. He knows that sin destroys us and that breaks His heart. That is how much God loves us.

Once again, I ask, do you feel encouraged and strengthened? When the world and people are weighing you down, remember these two things – He loves and He forgives you. Both are complete and cannot be changed.

If you are in Christ, you are loved and forgiven, period.

# Day 305

You are a Stone

Ezekiel 1:1-3:15 / Hebrews 3 / Psalm 104:1-23 / Proverbs 26:24-26

The Bible refers to us, as God's people, in many ways. We are called "sheep", "jars of clay", and "the bride." In Hebrews 3:6 we are told that we are His house. "But Christ is faithful as the Son over God's house. And we are His house if indeed we hold firmly to our confidence and the hope in which we glory."

There is another place in scripture that refers to God's people as a house.

1 Peter 2:4-5 says:

"You are coming to Christ, who is the living cornerstone of God's temple. He was rejected by people, but he was chosen by God for great honor. And you are living stones that God is building into his spiritual temple. What's more, you are his holy priests. Through the mediation of Jesus Christ, you offer spiritual sacrifices that please God."

We are called "living stones" which must be built together to form a spiritual temple or building. But we cannot even begin construction without Jesus as our "living cornerstone." A cornerstone in construction sets the initial placement of a building and causes the rest of the building to be square and stable. That perfectly describes what Jesus does in our lives.

The above analogies are interesting and easy to understand for me because both my husband Jeff and I have experience in the construction industry. Jeff is a residential contractor, and I worked both as a draftswoman for a construction company and as a cost estimator for a millwork company. I also took several classes in college that taught me about construction.

With Jesus as our cornerstone, we are being built together by Holy Spirit as a house for God's Spirit. As we're being built beside another stone, we don't necessarily fit easily together. What would a good mason do to ensure two stones fit together? He would do two things.

First, he would chisel off the rough edges so that the final structure is strong and pleasing to the eye. The chiseling comes when we learn to live together in love; forgiving one another as Christ Jesus has forgiven us (see Ephesians 4:32.) I didn't say it was always fun to be built together into a stone house!

Next, he would apply mortar so that the two stones bond. The mortar, I believe, is God's Spirit which cements us together in the unity that Jesus and the Father enjoyed. What does the verse mean that we are a house if we hold firmly to confidence and hope?

Confidence can be defined as, "Freedom in speaking, unreservedness in speech, openly, frankly, without concealment, free and fearless confidence, cheerful courage, boldness, etc." As you can see by these definitions, when we are being built alongside other Jesus followers, we must be bold to speak to God, ourselves, and one another. Why? Because your fellow Jesus followers need to be encouraged and given strength. That is part of what we must do for one another.

What about hope?

Hope is defined as, "Expectation of good, joyful and confident expectation of eternal salvation, and faith." Negativity will stop us short of the destiny God has. But hope in God, along with trusting in His promises and His Word will take us to the very end of our journey, and we'll be excited to arrive at our eternal reward with Him.

Day 306

The Door is Open

Ezekiel 3:16-6:14 / Hebrews 4 / Psalm 104:24-35 / Proverbs 26:27

Who remembers the game called Truth or Dare? If you're unfamiliar, the game is played with any number of people. Each person takes a turn being "it". The "it" person must be asked and must answer, "Do you choose truth? Or dare?" Then that person must either answer a question truthfully, or they must perform a daring task. I'm not saying this game is always a good idea! Sometimes it can cause embarrassment and/or physical harm!

The truth part of the game can be both revealing and scary. None of us exposes our hearts to others for fear of being rejected once we're known. If each of us knew the other people around us, we might be shocked, fearful, or disgusted. Or perhaps there are those who are truly honest and pure of heart, and those would cause us to experience deep conviction. That would not be a bad thing!

When Hebrews 4 talks about rest, which is most of the chapter, it is interesting to note that the topic of rest is followed by the role and effectiveness of the Word of God. Upon first reading, I wondered why one would follow the other, but as I read through a commentary, I realized the reason. Just like the game of Truth or Dare above, those around us are not always aware of the hidden things in our hearts; neither are we always aware of our own hearts.

So, while we may believe we have entered rest, or that those around us have entered God's rest, the Word of God is the light which exposes and instructs us on where our trust lies. What do I mean by that?

Hebrews 4:1 reads,

> "Therefore, since the promise of
> entering His rest still stands, let us be careful that
> none of you be found to have fallen short of it."

Verse one tells us that it's possible to miss the rest of God. We may miss His rest either by ignorance or deception. Once we know what it is to enter His rest, we have a choice. We may accept or reject what He has provided. I'll talk more about that in a minute.

The deception comes when we say we are resting, but within our hearts is a wrestling match that we don't want anyone to see. We may do this because we want to appear holy and mature. It would be better for us to be revealed as we are so we may grow. And don't fear showing up as you are because both your Father in Heaven and those who truly love you will be grateful for your courage and will fight to partner with you in your spiritual growth.

How is God's rest defined, and how do we know we have received that rest? God rested on the seventh day of creation because His work was finished. (Hebrews 4:4). When the Father sent His Son Jesus Christ to the earth, He sent Him to complete a work. That work was to go to the cross and shed His blood so our sins would be forgiven, and we could be reconciled in relationship to the Father. Jesus completed that work.

Jesus paid for our salvation, and He holds us firmly in His hand. He has completed all that needs to be done for our right standing with the Father. We have no work to accomplish toward this task.

Our rest comes when we receive the fact that Jesus paid it all.

Finished. Completed. Nothing for me to do, except trust Him, believe Him and enter His rest. Did you notice we enter "His" rest? It is a rest He has provided; all I must do is walk through the door and it is also my rest.

Then comes the role of God's Word in calling us into the rest (see Hebrews 4:12-13 for the role of the Word.) If we are tortured by fear, worry, or sin, we have not entered the rest Jesus Christ gave us. This is not to condemn anyone; this is to offer an opportunity to receive what He has done and live from a place of victory instead of a place of needing to accomplish just "one more thing" so we can be righteous.

> You are righteous through Jesus Christ.
> You are free in Him.
> You have rest, forgiveness, peace, and safety in Him.
> It is finished.

I implore you today to enter His rest. Just find the door – Jesus – and walk through. Sit down, grab a glass of water, and listen to His beautiful, life-giving Words.

Enjoy His rest today.

123

Day 307

As for Me and My Family

Ezekiel 7-9 / Hebrews 5 / Psalm 105:1-15 / Proverbs 26:28

Territory and property are marked and claimed in different ways. If you own a home and land, you have boundary lines that a surveyor measured and marked, and you have a deed to your property showing what you own. If you're married, you have a marriage certificate, and most people wear wedding rings, so others know they are "taken". If you were born in this country, you have a birth certificate that confirms your gender, age, and place of birth.

Everyone appreciates being identified, and allowing that identity to show to everyone who sees it that he is unique. There are probably many identifying factors and markings that one could claim, in addition to the ones I mentioned in the previous paragraph. One identifying mark is of utmost importance and that is an affirmation that we belong to Jesus Christ.

Most people, whether Christian or not, have heard of the mark of the beast, and most speak of it in hushed tones and with reverent fear. But did you know there is another biblical mark? I'll call it the mark of the righteous. I'm sure you want proof, so allow me to offer that.

In Ezekiel 9:3-4 this is what we read,

"Then the glory of the God of Israel rose up from between the cherubim, where it had rested, and moved to the entrance of the Temple. And the Lord called to the man dressed in linen who was carrying the writer's case. He said to him, 'Walk through the streets of Jerusalem and put a mark on the foreheads of all who weep and sigh because of the detestable sins being committed in their city.'"

There it is. A man dressed in linen who carried a writer's case was instructed to go through Jerusalem and put a mark on the forehead of all who hated sin. I'm guessing the writer's case included parchment, a quill of some kind, and ink. Instead of being fearful of the mark of the beast, I'm excited to know I have the mark of the righteous. How do I know if I bear that mark?

In the Old Testament, a man or woman either followed or ignored the law of God. Those who followed God's law were said to be righteous, and those who did not were referred to as the wicked. I'm assuming the man dressed in linen knew who was righteous as he walked through the streets.

What about you? What about pulling these questions into today's times? Are you one who weeps and sighs because of the detestable sins being committed in your city, state, nation, and the world? Are you aware that sins that are so horrible; sins I will not speak of here, are being committed under our very noses?

Sometime in April of 2020, the Lord said something life-changing to me. He told me this, "I want you to look into the dark areas around you because I need you to know what has been happening under your watch." I told the Lord I had an idea of what was happening and that I was afraid I would be overwhelmed with the evil and wickedness I would find. He urged me to open my eyes, take my head out of the sand, and see what I had avoided seeing.

So, I began a journey that I will not describe here. I began to search to find the answers to the horrible questions I knew God wanted me to know. I saw and heard things that broke my heart, made me sick, and made me wish the Lord had not asked me to see. But I obeyed Him.

It is now with a broken heart over the deep, dark sin across this earth that I spend time in prayer, asking God to purge evil, bring repentance and have mercy on those who are His.

During this time of awakening, a phrase came across my view. That phrase was, "God woke you up for a reason." And I know that's true. I am part of the remnant. I am one who stands in my generation as both a sentinel and a beacon. The sentinel says, "You shall not pass!" and the beacon says, "This is the way God would have you walk."

God knows who I am because I have come into right relationship with the Father through the Son Jesus Christ.

I have a mark on my forehead. Do you? Do you want a mark on your forehead? Can I tell you a secret? You will have one mark or the other. Maybe the better question is, "Do you want the mark of the beast or the mark of the righteous?" I want to leave you with these two verses.

"So fear the Lord and serve him wholeheartedly. Put away forever the idols your ancestors worshiped when they lived beyond the Euphrates River and in Egypt. Serve the Lord alone.

"But if you refuse to serve the Lord, then choose today whom you will serve. Would you prefer the gods your ancestors served beyond the Euphrates? Or will it be the gods of the Amorites in whose land you now live? But as for me and my family, we will serve the Lord." — Joshua 24:14-15

127

Day 308

Do Not Lose Heart

Ezekiel 10-11 / Hebrews 6 / Psalm 105:16-36 / Proverbs 27:1-2

Doctor's offices, grocery store lines, auto mechanic's shops, customer service calls; all these places have the potential to cause frustration. Why? Because all of them involve waiting, one of our favorite (not) things to do! There are times I'll avoid these places and situations simply because I dread waiting. There are several examples in scripture where God gave promises and then people had to wait for the promises to be fulfilled.

One person who had to wait was Joseph. If you remember the story of Joseph, you remember that God had given him dreams as a young man. In the dreams, the sun, moon, and stars were bowing down to him. He probably thought the dreams would be fulfilled the next day. He certainly was not expecting to be taken into Egypt as a slave.

In Hebrews, we read about another man who had to wait for something that had been promised. The part I want to explore is the way in which he waited. This is what Hebrews 6:15 says,

"And so after waiting patiently,
Abraham received what was promised."

We have two options when waiting. One, we can be impatient and frustrated. Or two, we can wait patiently, finding something to occupy our time in the meanwhile. The word "patiently" from the Merriam-Webster dictionary means "In a patient manner: with calmness or without complaint or hurry in spite of delays, difficulties, tedium, etc."

In the King James version, this verse says, "After he had patiently endured..." Now let's define the words "patiently endured" from the Strong's Concordance.

"To be long spirited, forbearing, or patient; to be longsuffering, to have long patience."

It can also mean,

"Not to lose heart, to persevere patiently, and bravely, in enduring misfortunes and troubles, to be patient in bearing the offenses and injuries of others, to be mild and slow in avenging, to be long-suffering, slow to anger, slow to punish."

In looking at all these definitions, I see the potential for a manual to be written on becoming more Christ-like as we patiently wait. I sincerely believe I could study this one verse and definition for an entire year. The reason I say an entire year is because after we study and understand, we must apply the verse to our lives. James 2:14-26 talks about how faith without works is dead.

Let's explore what it means not to lose heart by reading 2 Thessalonians 3:13.

"As for you, brethren, do not grow weary in doing good."
—New King James Version.

It can be difficult to maintain a good attitude when no one appreciates our effort. God has blessed us with so many good things, and He expects us to take care of what He's given us.

When we follow Jesus, we must be the first to be fed from the good things God has given us. If you are not full, you have nothing to give to anyone else. The initial blessing belongs to you, and the overflow belongs to others. Please do not mix those two up by giving your blessings away to others. Keep the blessings and give away the abundance, or the part that spills out from your life. Then you will never "go hungry" and you will never "lose heart."

May you be filled and also overflow so that all your needs, as well as the needs of those around you, will be met by the Lord!

131

Day 309

We Have Only One Priest

Ezekiel 12:1-14:11 / Hebrews 7:1-17 / Psalm 105:37-45 / Proverbs 27:3

Religion is an interesting topic. Religion is defined by Merriam Webster as: "An organized system of beliefs, ceremonies, and rules used to worship a god or a group of gods." Each religion names its god and has certain ways that god demands to be worshiped. I am not fully familiar with every aspect of religions other than Christianity, although I know a little about several belief systems.

Instead of studying the other religions and their gods, I want to focus on the truth found in the Christian faith. Feel free to compare by implication with other religions you have familiarity with. In Christianity, we do not work to earn our salvation. Jesus Christ has fully paid the price for our salvation by His death on the cross, His burial, and His resurrection and ascension back to Heaven.

In Christianity, we are not required to offer sacrifices, offerings of food or incense, or subject ourselves to bodily harm or injury. Jesus Christ is our sacrifice, and the old system of animal sacrifice was done away with. If you know a religion that practices blood sacrifice, you can be assured this religion does not lead to life.

In Christianity, we are not required to observe certain days to make ourselves holy. We are holy through the blood Jesus Christ shed on the cross, and this gift of holiness allows us to approach the Father in Heaven. We are given free access to the Father through the Son, Jesus Christ. We no longer require someone to mediate between us and God, such as a priest. That is because Jesus has become our priest.

It is this last point of Jesus Christ being our priest who allows us access to the Father that I want to talk more about. Hebrews 7 has several references to Jesus Christ as Messiah and priest. For example, in verse 11b,

> "Why was there still need for another priest to come,
> one in the order of Melchizedek,
> not in the order of Aaron?" (NIV)

Aaron was from the tribe of Levi out of which all priests came. Jesus, referred to as from the order of Melchizedek, was from the tribe of Judah. Yet he was still referred to as a priest.

Hebrews 7:16 says of Jesus,

> "One who has become a priest
> not on the basis of a regulation as to his ancestry
> but on the basis of the power
> of an indestructible life." (NIV)

The priesthood of Jesus was ordained by God, and Jesus who was God in the flesh lived a perfect, sinless life. This makes Him alone our perfect high priest through whom we may approach God.

In Christianity, we are allowed direct access to the one God who created all things through the Son Jesus Christ. Jesus was a unique son who was fully God yet lowered Himself into the form of man so that He might save us from death. No other religion allows direct access to the deity.

The other religions I've learned about require something of the followers yet offer little to nothing in return. Followers of other religions require sacrifices of different kinds, observances of all sorts, and perhaps the follower is given a measure of peace and hope in the practice. However, any acts a man or woman can offer will never remove the guilt of sin and punishment of death.

There is only one way to escape sin and death, and it has nothing to do with what we have done, or anything we will do to make ourselves righteous, or right with God. We cannot make ourselves righteous. I understand that what I'm sharing will only be received if the Holy Spirit is present to reveal to our hearts the truth. So, I pray that those who read this entry will have the gift of Holy Spirit enlightening their hearts and minds toward truth.

If you have attempted to earn your salvation, or even to keep your salvation or to be righteous apart from what God has provided, may Holy Spirit lift the veil from your eyes and heart and may you be able to see and to hear truth. Jesus Christ is the only way to the Father (John 14:6.) He is the only door. He is the only escape. Run to Him and be saved!

Day 310

A Faithful Friend is Rare

Ezekiel 14:12-16:41 / Hebrews 7:18-28
Psalm 106:1-12 / Proverbs 27:4-6

If we had siblings, they were our first best friends. But boy, oh, boy could they be annoying! I remember loving my sister and brother so much, but I also remember some terrible squabbles. When we went on long car rides, we used to tussle over how much space we each had in the back seat. So, my parents would draw imaginary dividing lines between us and dare us to cross them! That helped a little...

Sadly, my "bratty little brother" has already moved on to Heaven. I would give anything for one more squabble. My sister and I left fighting behind many years ago. We are to the point now where we simply agree to disagree, or we find common ground realizing fighting serves no beneficial purpose.

However, there are times when family or friends will say something, either intentionally, or not realizing it, that cuts us to the core. We know they are right, but we certainly don't want to hear it! Sometimes our immediate reaction is to dismiss their words because we are certain they're mistaken.

Even if we initially believe the words could not apply to us, if we're wise, we'll consider what was said. Praying about what was said is even more valuable. Usually when someone speaks, there is an element of some truth to what they are sharing. Either they have seen a behavior, or heard words come from our mouths that do not line up with who they know us to be.

If that family member or friend loves us, they should either find a way to share, or pray God shows us. I've read Proverbs 27:6 many times but have not always been happy about the words.

"Wounds from a friend can be trusted,
but an enemy multiplies kisses."

Wounds don't sound fun whether they are from a friend or an enemy. The Strong's Concordance is helpful with understanding the word for "wounds". That definition is, "To wound by bruising or to wound by crushing." Yes, I realize this still does not sound like fun.

I have long had the understanding that it is the mercy of God that will not leave us in our sin. Why? Because God understands that sin destroys our lives, bringing death to every area of our hearts; both emotionally and physically. In His mercy, He corrects and disciplines us. It is this same thought process with which I read Proverbs 27:6.

I believe that God uses the mercy and love of our friends to speak truth into our lives so that we will not be wrecked by sin. Sin has consequences and all those consequences lead to death. One may believe she is immune from reaping what she is sowing, but that is never true. Something will always follow our actions, whether positive or negative.

It breaks God's heart to see us gather negative consequences into our lives. I believe our friends who see us caught up in sin feel the same way. I know my heart has been grieved for a family member or friend who is following that wide path of destruction that leads to death. The one walking the path does not always see the end. Others in our lives can oftentimes see what we cannot.

So, if a friend speaks to you, it is the love and mercy of God toward you that they are risking your anger and rejection to try to help you. You may not be thankful for them right away. But hopefully, you'll eventually see that they put their hearts on the line for your sake. They did what they did because they love you so much. Be gracious. Receive the correction and thank God for such a beautiful friend!

Day 311

Bring Joy to the Heart

Ezekiel 16:42-17:24 / Hebrews 8 / Psalm 106:13-31 / Proverbs 27:7-9

What kinds of things make you happy, or bring you joy? If I were to ask that question of my family and friends, I might have hundreds of different responses, ranging from food to people, and from the natural sounds of nature to the soft green grass underfoot. However, I also believe I would find a trend where several answered similarly. I would guess that those we love and who love us would bring the greatest joy to our hearts. So, somewhere in the answers would be one loved person or another.

Yesterday, we talked about the wounds of a faithful friend. Today, I want to talk about the joy that the same friend brings. Let's refer to this topic as the "other side of the coin." Both sides of this coin have value, but this side will be the sweeter side. If the other side of the coin may have caused us pain, this side will bring the needed healing.

Proverbs 27:9 in The Passion Translation tells us this,

"Perfume and incense bring joy to the heart,
and the pleasantness of a friend
springs from their heartfelt advice."

Words such as perfume, incense, joy, pleasantness, and heartfelt are all intended to make one feel loved and safe. In biblical times perfume and incense often referred to oils that were distilled from the many plants available in each area. God designed the plants, trees, and fruits not only for eating, shade, and wood for building, among other uses, but He also intended for us to use these things for the healing of our souls and bodies.

In February 2015 I was introduced to the world of essential oils and other products made with these healing oils. Since that time, I've enjoyed the purity and body-supporting properties of these amazing smelling substances. I have so many favorite oils now. Two of my favorites, and it's hard to choose just two, are lemon and Valor essential oils.

I refer to lemon essential oil as, "daddy oil" because my daddy loved all things made from lemon, such as lemon meringue pie, lemon bars, etc. Valor essential oil is a blend of several oils, that are combined and bring me courage and deep comfort. So, when verse 9 says that perfume and incense bring "Joy to the heart," I can attest that I've experienced that.

The comparison of these amazing scents bringing joy, and the heartfelt advice from a friend also bringing pleasantness, is easy to understand. Who doesn't enjoy sitting with a trusted friend and hearing words of comfort and affirmation? I know I need those words at times. I will admit to being one who receives those words rarely, but when they do come, they bring joy to my heart.

I've heard some say that we shouldn't speak too well of others because we'll give them a "big head." I don't agree with that assessment. I am convinced that all of us are bombarded by so much negativity daily that we require words of affirmation to fill that empty tank.

As negativity drains us, the words of affirmation, especially from our Father in Heaven, are water to our souls.

I encourage you to let your first friend be the Father. Allow Him to affirm and fill you with His words of life. Then if you receive life-giving words from others, that will be your bonus encouragement! I also want to challenge you to remember to speak about the good things you're hearing to others. Oftentimes, we think about something good but forget to speak it aloud. Remember to say those words and encourage your friend!

143

Day 312

Are You the Preacher?

Ezekiel 18-19 / Hebrews 9:1-10 / Psalm 106:32-48 / Proverbs 27:10

This morning as the Lord and I talked together; I heard Him tell me that He would love for me to look for His true nature as I read scripture. He said He wants me to know His heart according to what His Word says and not according to what I've heard second-hand. So, as I read, I listened for evidence of His heart, and I found a great truth that applies well to our season in history.

Ezekiel 18:23 and 32 reads (NIV Version,)

> "Do I take any pleasure in the death of the wicked?
> declares the Sovereign Lord. Rather, am I not pleased
> when they turn from their ways and live?"

And

> "For I take no pleasure in the death of anyone,
> declares the Sovereign Lord. Repent and live!"

God is asking a question, and when God asks a question, be assured that He already knows the answer. If one doubts the answer to His question on whether He takes pleasure in the death of the wicked, keep reading until you reach verse 32 and the answer is clear. He takes no pleasure in the death of anyone.

I've noticed a trend on social media where some seem to rejoice in the misfortune or even the death of another. That has always hurt my heart so deeply. Some believe that it's better for evil people to die and leave the earth, and I understand the intention behind that: to rid the earth of evil.

However, we must remember that those evil people are valued by God. Maybe you're wondering why God would value someone that society sees as evil. I get that. But, since we are not God, and we cannot see into a person's heart, we don't know what may be transpiring between them and God.

All of us will die one day. Some of us will enter eternity having been found in Christ, and some will enter eternity having rejected the gift of Salvation offered by Jesus' death on the cross. So, while some are rejoicing at the death of another, God is not.

That proves to me that His heart of love is larger, deeper, and wider than any human love could ever reach. That person you hate, that one you haven't forgiven, that one you talk about behind her back, Jesus loves that one. That means we should also love her and others like her.

If God takes no pleasure in the death of anyone, neither should we! I realize this may be hard to swallow, but would you as a follower of Christ honestly be okay with another human being, created in God's image, spending all eternity in hell? If so, then it's time for a heart check. Our hearts must be broken for those who are lost without Christ. We should both love them and pray for their salvation.

Yes, even the most evil and vile human you know needs the Savior. Might that evil person reject Jesus Christ? Yes, they might. But if someone has been brought across your path, God expects you to love that one and to pray for her salvation. If you get an opportunity to share your faith, include that as well because…

Romans 10:14 in the NIV states,

"How, then, can they call on the one they have not believed in? And how can they believe in the one of whom they have not heard? And how can they hear without someone preaching to them?"

Have you ever considered that you may be someone's preacher? Follow the heart of the Father, pray, love, and share truth. You might just see someone's destiny changed!

Day 313

Jesus is No Copycat!

Ezekiel 20 / Hebrews 9:11-28 / Psalm 107 / Proverbs 27:11

You've probably heard someone say that the Spirit realm is more real than the natural realm. I've heard that said. Maybe they don't mean "more real." Perhaps they intend to agree that the Spirit realm is everlasting while the earth and the natural realm will one day pass away. Yes, God's Word says that our current heaven and earth will pass away and that a new heaven and earth will be brought down from Heaven. (Revelation 21:1)

Along these same lines, when God instructed Moses to build the tabernacle while the descendants of Israel wandered in the desert, it was with the understanding that God was having the people build a replica of the dwelling place of God in Heaven.

I've heard other parallels that suggest that the things we see on the earth are replicas of what exists in Heaven. I've heard some say the Garden of Eden is a replica.

Fascinating!

I believe God desires to meet with us and walk with us like He did Adam and Eve before sin entered the world. I hope you hear Him as He draws your heart into that place. There is nothing sweeter than to sit in God's presence and exchange conversation with Him. You'll hear the most amazing and beautiful things!

Today, as I read in Hebrews 9, I was in awe of the description of Jesus entering the tabernacle in Heaven by the means of His own perfect blood. (Please read Hebrews 9:11-28 from the devotional today!) We are so far removed from the Old Testament and the historical account of having to offer animal sacrifices for sin. I'm thankful we no longer operate under that covenant.

Reading about the old covenant and all it required makes me even more thankful for the willing sacrifice of Jesus on the cross so that our sins could be forgiven. I realize that the topic of blood sacrifices being required also seems odd to many. If you'll remember the first blood sacrifice required for the first sin; Adam and Eve were tricked by the serpent and ate from the forbidden tree. Once they ate, they realized they were naked: their sin-nature was awakened, and they needed to be clothed.

God killed an animal to cover them and so, it began.

I won't dive too deeply into the counterfeits of the enemy but will only mention that the devil has his own copycat forms of blood sacrifice. Perhaps some are aware of this, and some are not. I will not go into any detail as to give no glory to the enemy. Suffice it to say, that the devil copies everything God originates. Always keep that in mind when studying scripture and when looking at practices today.

Let's look at the imagery of verse 11 together; it's too beautiful not to mention!

"But when Christ came as high priest of the good things that are now already here, He went through the greater and more perfect tabernacle that is not made with human hands..."

Then look at verse 23.

"It was necessary, then, for the copies of the heavenly things to be purified with these sacrifices, but the heavenly things themselves with better sacrifices than these."

And verse 24 says:

"For Christ did not enter a sanctuary made with human hands that was only a copy of the true one, He entered heaven itself, now to appear for us in God's presence. New International Version

That last part destroys my heart, in a good way! Jesus Christ entered heaven and appeared before God for us! If that doesn't humble you to your knees... No more blood sacrifices were required after that. Jesus Christ paid the debt for our sin in full. I don't have to do anything except believe in and declare the Name of Jesus Christ.

He is my Savior and Lord, and He has made me His beloved. I don't know if any of us fully realizes the gift we have been given. But I pray that as you read, Holy Spirit will reveal the Father's heart to you. May you be overwhelmed by His love today.

151

Day 314

Confident Christ Followers

Ezekiel 21-22 / Hebrews 10:1-17 / Psalm 108 / Proverbs 27:12

How many of you have ever felt insecure about anything? I know I have. Insecure, lacking in confidence, uncertain or unsure; all these words describe our hearts at times. Sometimes we just don't know what to do or how to respond in a situation, and we've all felt this way. Even the most secure-looking or sounding person has situations in which she is unsure of herself.

I believe we will be insecure if we put our trust in the wrong thing or person. I've heard people say, "I don't trust anyone but myself!" May I say that trusting yourself is dangerous! You are imperfect. You have days when you know what to do and days when you are bewildered by the dealings in life.

Do you always rely on your own ideas and wisdom? Do you ever ask someone else for their input or opinions? What about God? Have you ever asked for His input, opinions, or answers to your questions? Wisdom is hard to come by - at least true wisdom: the kind that provides a solid foundation so that we feel secure about our next move.

Psalm 108:1 (NIV) has a word that will revolutionize your life and mine. So, I want to share the word with you!

First, here is the verse:

> "My heart is confident in you,
> O God; no wonder I can sing
> Your praises with all my heart!"

Have you ever been so confident that you were singing at the top of your lungs? Or have you ever met someone who is that confident? That is the picture that develops in my mind when I read this verse. Most of us hide when we sing. Why? Maybe we can't carry a tune, or maybe we are afraid of what others will think.

I believe God is blessed and pleased when we are confident enough in Him to let loose with praise, songs, laughter, or whatever expression is on our hearts. The word I want to further study is "confident," and as we have so often discovered when studying the meaning of other words, this word is also full of beautiful meaning.

The word confident means:

"To be firm, be stable, be established, to be set up, be fixed, be secure, be enduring, be securely determined, to be directed aright, be steadfast in a moral sense, to prepare, be ready, be arranged, and be restored."

I didn't list every definition, but I did pull out most of the meanings. However, even from this list, you can see the strength of this word: "My heart is confident in You, O God." Imagine if Jesus Christ were your foundation. I ask you to imagine it that way because the word confidence strikes me as a very foundational word.

I believe if we are confident, according to the definitions above, there will be nothing we cannot accomplish through God's Spirit. If confidence in God is my foundation, I can certainly build anything of weight upon it. It will neither crumble nor collapse.

When I'm building by the Spirit, I am listening to His instructions while using His tools to build. My gifts and talents will be fully used because I will be operating according to my God-design. Once we know who we are in Christ, both as a general follower and as an individual, we will be able to confidently live our lives the way He purposed. We will rule on the earth, we will share truth, and we will see others go free. Confidence is a huge asset in our Christian life.

If you do not currently feel confident, I invite you to open your heart to Jesus Christ and listen to Him to find the path He has already established by His Spirit inside you. Once you're on that path, listen to His instructions. As you follow Him, He will do the hard part. Remember that our job is to believe in Jesus Christ and to speak the truth in love. The rest is up to Him!

155

Day 315

A Bath for the Soul

Ezekiel 23 / Hebrews 10:18-39 / Psalm 109 / Proverbs 27:13

Each of us takes a bath or shower at regular intervals: at least we all hope you do. If you've studied history, you're aware that back in the old days when water had to be carried from a water source and heated on the stove to fill the big tub, baths were only on Saturday night before church on Sundays. Yea, there were some stinky people back then. That was also before deodorant was invented, although I'm sure they had ways to try to cut down on the smell.

Did you know that the saying, "Don't throw the baby out with the bathwater" came from this period in history? We learned about this when we went to historic Williamsburg, VA several years ago. One of the actors shared where some of our sayings came from. From the way I remember it, the man of the house got the first bath, then the sons, then the wife, then the daughters, and the baby was last.

By the time the baby got into the same water everyone else had used, it was not only filled with soap, but it was also very dirty. So, it might be easy to miss the baby if it was still in the water. No, we're not talking about accidentally drowning babies! The saying was to be sure you had gotten the baby washed and out of the tub before you emptied the water, thus: "Throwing the baby out with the bathwater."

Today, that saying has a different meaning. There are some in my life who tend to throw out the proverbial baby, meaning they miss the point of the conversation or the intended meaning at hand, and in disgust or offense, throw out the entire idea or conversation as worthless. This tends to happen when a conversation requires more thought and work to get ideas across to the other person. Some don't want to or have time for the hard work of conversing toward understanding.

All that to say, one of today's verses got me thinking about these baths. Hebrews 10:22b in the NIV tells us,

> "For our guilty consciences have been sprinkled
> with Christ's blood to make us clean, and our bodies
> have been washed with pure water."

Now, do you see why I thought of those baths?

The baths we take are for our physical bodies to be clean; but how is that different from our bodies being washed with this pure water from scripture? The scriptural body washing refers to our baptism after or along with salvation. Baptism with water symbolizes a washing having taken place inside us. Baptism is also a public declaration of our faith and desire to follow Jesus Christ.

Water by itself does not make a person clean in a spiritual sense; the Holy Spirit must invade us for the process of becoming like Christ to begin. What about the part of the blood of Christ making our guilty conscience clean? We are guilty when we've done something wrong, or when we've sinned. Sin separates us from our loving heavenly Father.

When our conscience is made clean because of Jesus's work on the cross, we are free to choose good things. It is our conscience that causes us to choose between good and evil. Our guilty conscience is the alert system telling us we have sinned and need to be forgiven. When our conscience has been washed, we are relieved from guilt.

Salvation allows us to be washed in our spirits, our souls, and our bodies: meaning at salvation our spirits are made perfect because Jesus Christ comes to live there. Then our souls are made clean as we submit to Holy Spirit's work. Finally, our bodies will be made new when we enter eternity to live with God. That is our final washing.

The next time you take a bath; I encourage you to reflect on the washing of the Holy Spirit and thank Him for making you spiritually clean.

159

Day 316

Activate Your Faith

Ezekiel 24-26 / Hebrews 11:1-16 / Psalm 110 / Proverbs 27:14

Faith is one of those topics that is so wide-ranging we could never cover it all in one entry. However, I still want to talk about faith today. How can one not talk about faith when reading through Hebrews 11? It is, after all, referred to by many as the faith chapter.

Verse 1 begins with defining faith as, "The reality of what we hope for; the evidence of things we cannot see." As I enjoy doing, I want to look at the definition of faith according to Merriam Webster's Dictionary. Faith is defined as, "A strong belief or trust in something or someone."

When looking at Abraham's life, Romans 4:3 tells us,

> "Abraham believed God, and God
> counted him as righteous because of his faith."

Do you understand that faith and believing God are the same? We have each been given a measure of faith by God (Romans 12:3). That means our initial faith is a gift from God and not something we've earned.

What does that gift of faith allow us to do? It allows us to believe God. When we read our Bibles or hear Holy Spirit speaking to us, we will have some ability to believe what we're hearing. But sometimes there are things in our souls that keep us from being able to believe; these things are called soul wounds. Soul wounds can keep us from believing the truth we are hearing from God.

Sometimes our gift of faith can be covered in "mud" (the wounds), not allowing us to receive the grace and truth God wants to bring. Therefore, if we are having a hard time believing the truth of God's Word, we need to ask Him to show us what needs to be healed in our souls. Once our souls are healed in an area, we will once again be able to use the gift of faith we've been given to take God at His Word.

As we continue to believe what God says in His Word, we will continue to be healed and to be encouraged. We will also find ourselves being changed into the image of Jesus Christ. Then we can begin modeling the type of life Jesus led on earth. The life where we actively choose the will of the Father as Jesus did.

Another aspect of faith is that it causes us to act. We cannot say we have faith if we do not have an action to follow that faith. I can say I have the faith to get a new job, but if I never fill out an application or go on an interview, I will not get a new job.

James 2:14 proves the necessity of our actions.

"What good is it, dear brothers, and sisters,
if you say you have faith but don't show it by your actions?
Can that kind of faith save anyone?"

Romans 10:17 says this,

"So, faith comes from hearing, that is,
hearing the Good News about Christ."

If your faith does not feel active, perhaps you need to hear more of the Good News. The Good News is the Gospel regarding Jesus

Christ's birth, death, burial, and resurrection. The instruction of the entire body of Scripture that proves the nature of our loving, powerful Father is also necessary for our faith to be made active.

If our faith has gone to sleep through misuse or neglect, I believe we need our faith to be made active again. The gift of faith is within you since you have received Him. Activate that gift again by reading God's Word, and through conversation with Him.

He wants your faith to be strong and active so that you will fulfill all He intends for you, and so that others will see the light of Christ through your life.

Day 317

My Faith in Action

Ezekiel 27-28 / Hebrews 11:17-31 / Psalm 111 / Proverbs 27:15-16

Yesterday we talked about faith. Today we're going to talk a little more about faith, so maybe we'll call this entry "Faith, Part 2." Since faith is so foundational to all we are and all we do as the people of God, I believe two days of discussion are valuable for this topic.

Yesterday, I mentioned to you from James 2:20b that: "Faith without works is dead." (KJV) I want to talk more about this aspect of faith today.

Even before I read Hebrews 11 in the NIV, Holy Spirit brought a fascinating thought to my mind. He said to me, "Watch what happens as you read. Each person will be said to have faith, and each statement of faith will be followed by something they did." My mind started racing as I read.

I want to go over with you the list of what each person named in this passage did in response to the fact that they believed what God had said.

Abraham believed God, so he offered his son Isaac.

Isaac believed God, so he promised blessings for his sons Jacob and Esau.

Jacob believed God, so he blessed each of Joseph's sons and bowed in worship as he leaned on his staff.

Joseph believed God, so he told the people of God they would leave Egypt, and he commanded them to take his bones with them when they left.

Moses' parents believed God, so they hid him for three months when he was born.

Moses believed God, so he refused to be called the son of Pharaoh's daughter.

Moses believed God again, so he left the land of Egypt.

Moses believed God again, so he commanded the people of Israel to keep the Passover.

The people of Israel believed God, so they went right through the Red Sea.

The people of Israel believed God again, so they marched around Jericho for seven days, and the walls came crashing down.

Rahab believed God, so she gave a friendly welcome to the spies.

We can no longer deny that believing God must be followed by an action of some kind. So, I must ask, what are you believing God for? What are you doing about what you believe?

I am believing God for an increase in my influence as a spiritual mom and prophetic voice, so I have remodeled my art studio and office space to match the measure He is speaking to me in the Spirit. The space is beyond my wildest dreams; it's so beautiful!

I have a new desk, a new large window, space for my books (I love to read), an area for all my art projects (I am an artist), and my office has many beautiful spaces from which to shoot pictures and video so I can bring you the messages God puts on my heart.

I believe God has called me to this lifestyle of equipping and encouraging others. I believe God has spoken prosperity over my family in this season, so I am preparing to receive what God has spoken. I want to encourage you to hear God, dream big, and then plan and prepare for Him to pour Himself out in abundance over you, your family, your business, your ministry, or any other area He shows you!

Have faith: believe God: take action!

Day 318

Keep Running; Keep Fighting!

Ezekiel 29-30 / Hebrews 11:32-12:13 / Psalm 112 / Proverbs 27:17

When my daddy left earth (yes, I realize I speak of him often; he was an amazing person!), I first laughed because I knew he was seeing the face of his Savior, then I bawled because I am a daddy's girl to my very core. I miss him every single day, but I am so rich because of all he poured into me. Was he perfect? No. I could recount his faults, but why bother? He left an imprint, a mark, and a legacy on my soul.

I am who I am because of who he was. He was full of faith, passionate for Jesus and people, as stubborn as an old mule, and could tell the silliest jokes. He was artistic and creative, sensitive, and passionate. You did not tell him he couldn't do something because he would prove you wrong! All that sounds a lot like me. And I'm very proud to be known in these ways.

As we've read through Hebrews 11, I've realized that this is one of my favorite portions of Scripture. There are other scriptures that set my soul on fire, and this chapter is right up there with those. I love reading about the faith of our ancestors. I love reading about how their faith caused them to act, to obey, to move. I love knowing that they lived by faith until the very end.

I will be in that great cloud of witnesses one day. My daddy is in that great cloud now, cheering me on. When he left earth, I didn't realize that he would become one of those faithful witnesses in that great cloud. I mistakenly thought that cloud was only for the people in the Bible. But that is incorrect.

That great cloud has been being added to for centuries with the faithful lovers of God. I can't tell you how many are in the cloud of witnesses but it's a vast number. I remember when I first became aware that my daddy was standing there in heaven cheering me on. It was a powerful moment of realization. I knew I was carrying on his work and legacy, and I knew that he was urging me toward the goal.

What is the goal? Philippians 3 is powerful in answering that question. I encourage you to read the whole chapter. For time and space's sake, I will include only verses 12-14 from TPT.

"I admit that I haven't yet acquired the absolute fullness that I'm pursuing, but I run with passion into His abundance so that I may reach the purpose for which Christ Jesus laid hold of me to make me His own. I don't depend on my own strength to accomplish this; however, I do have one compelling focus: I forget all of the past as I fasten my heart to the future instead. I run straight for the divine invitation of reaching the heavenly goal and gaining the victory-prize through the anointing of Jesus."

Once again, my heart is on fire with the truth and passion included in these three verses! The six goals found in these verses are absolute fullness, reaching my purpose, forgetting the past, fastening my heart to the future, running toward His invitation to Heaven, and gaining the victory-prize.

Therefore, we fight. Therefore, we run. Therefore, we do not give up when life is hard. We are running to reach Heaven and be with our Father, Savior, and Friend. We are running so others will also be encouraged to run. We must not faint. We must not give up.

Day 319

Watch Over Each Other

Ezekiel 31-32 / Hebrews 12:14-29
Psalm 113-114 / Proverbs 27:18-20

Having relationships with others and choosing to be in community takes work. Sometimes when a relationship or friendship is new, everyone is on her or his best behavior and everything is peachy. But then the trials come, or the hidden hurts in another's soul show up. That's where the trouble can begin if we're unaware of how to walk with ourselves and others through the wounds of the past.

Yes, many of us have worked hard to heal the wounds and we've moved past many injustices and abuses, but there will likely always be at least one more wound we have forgotten, buried, or that we were not aware of carrying. That's when we must have grace for ourselves and those we love. The warts are going to be revealed.

Hebrews 12:14-15 in TPT offers some hard-hitting instructions to help us navigate relationships.

"In every relationship be swift to choose peace over competition, and run swiftly toward holiness, for those who are not holy will not see the Lord. Watch over each other to make sure that no one misses the revelation of God's grace. And make sure no one lives with a root of bitterness sprouting within them which will only cause trouble and poison the hearts of many."

Let's work through these two verses phrase by phrase for a better understanding. What does it mean to, "Be swift to choose peace over competition?" We should always turn our backs on sin, especially when it involves the way we treat others. We are not in competition with one another. What does the word "peace" mean?

> Peace is the Hebrew word "shalom." This word means much more than peace. It means "wholeness, wellness, well-being, safe, happy, friendly, favor, completeness, to make peace, peace offering, secure, to prosper, to be victorious, to be content, tranquil, quiet, and restful."

Shalom is used to describe those of us who have been provided with all that is needed to be whole and complete and break off all authority that would attempt to bind us to chaos.

Some followers of Christ work to be at peace with all others, and some are unaware of how to accomplish this. It does take work to be in a healthy relationship with each other, as stated above. But the rewards for that work are well worth the effort!

What does it mean to "run swiftly toward holiness?" This is a personal charge because we cannot run for someone else. When we run toward holiness, we are running toward consecration, purification, and sanctification. Let's define those three big words.

> Consecration is "the devoting or setting apart of anything to the worship or service of God." (From the Bible Dictionary.)

> Purification is "to free from guilt or moral or ceremonial blemish." (From the Merriam Webster Dictionary.)

> Sanctification is "to sanctify someone or something is to set that person or thing apart for the use intended by its designer." (From the Bible Dictionary.)

The last thing I want to define is the "root of bitterness." The Free Dictionary defines bitterness as, "anger and disappointment at being treated unfairly, resentment."

We are to guard our own hearts against bitterness through forgiveness and grace. How might we guard others against bitterness? I believe Holy Spirit will show us if there is a problem that we could help remedy by conversation and asking forgiveness. If you've caused a breach in a relationship, never be hesitant to communicate and make things right with another.

We must always remember that we don't live in a vacuum. All that we do affects us as well as those around us. Our choices and behavior will certainly produce either life or death in us. However, our choices and behavior can produce the same results in others. Therefore, we should live in a way that considers others and not just ourselves.

Day 320

Receive Inner Strength

Ezekiel 33-34 / Hebrews 13 / Psalm 115 / Proverbs 27:21-22

Think of the strongest person you know. Hercules, or maybe Marvel superheroes like The Hulk, Captain America, or even your dad or mom. What about your friend who lost her husband, or who survived after a scary diagnosis? Strength takes different forms. Some people are strong physically, some are strong mentally, emotionally, and/or spiritually.

Then there are times we don't feel strong at all, in any of those areas mentioned. Has anyone ever told you how they admire your strength, when they don't realize you're crumbling on the inside? A fake smile or a seemingly happy appearance can sometimes hide incredible pain.

But what if you could have true strength? A strength at your core; a strength that truly sustains you when hard times come, because hard times will always be with us. All of us want to feel confident, stable, and unshaken, especially when difficult things happen to us. I'm not talking about a kind of strength that doesn't allow us to feel, process, or be in the moment. We all need to be present in life.

I found two verses in today's reading that grabbed my attention because I feel I'm often in need of true strength. I need strength in my inner man (or woman.)

Hebrews 13:8 9 says,

"Jesus Christ is the same yesterday, today, and forever. So do not be attracted by strange, new ideas. Your strength comes from

God's grace, not from rules about food, which don't help those who follow them."

There were certain people in Jesus' day, and there are still some today, who believed they were more righteous because of what they did or didn't eat or drink. There were rules about not eating meat with blood still in it, and about not eating or drinking anything that had been sacrificed to idols. But as we've talked about before, it is not what we do and don't do that makes us righteous.

We are made righteous through the blood of Jesus Christ. We are made right with God when we choose to believe Him, which is faith. Some see themselves as better than others for the practices they follow, but in verse 9, Holy Spirit is telling us that our strength comes from God's grace.

"Strength" in this verse means, "to make firm, establish, confirm, and make sure." This definition reminds me of a scripture God gave me personally in 1998.

1 Peter 5:10 says:

"In his kindness God called you to share in his eternal glory by means of Christ Jesus. So, after you have suffered a little while, he will restore, support, and strengthen you, and he will place you on a firm foundation."

The word used for "strengthen," as used in 1 Peter 5:10, means "to make one's soul strong." The word "grace" means "the merciful kindness by which God, exerting his holy influence upon souls, turns them to Christ, keeps, strengthens, increases them in Christian faith, knowledge, affection, and kindles them to the exercise of the Christian virtues."

I want to share one final verse with you; it's the one I mentioned above.

Ephesians 3:16:

"I pray that from his glorious, unlimited resources
he will empower you with inner strength
through his Spirit."

It is the inner strength brought to us by God's empowering grace that makes us truly strong. There is nothing wrong with being physically strong, as a matter of fact, physical strength is necessary. However, if we are physically strong without being strong in our inner person, we are imbalanced and will not have everything we need.

177

Day 321

Patient Endurance

Ezekiel 35-36 / James 1:1-18 / Psalm 116 / Proverbs 27:23-27

I have talked from time to time about hard times, trials, difficulties, etc. No one really wants to talk about the sad or bad things that happen, but maybe we should. If we talk about them, maybe we can find purpose in them. No one would voluntarily sign up for trials; you'd have to be crazy to volunteer for that. But what we gain out of them is priceless.

So, what do we gain? Because if there is no benefit while we're going through the tough stuff, I'd just as soon pass on those experiences. James 1 is a challenging chapter of the Bible. The whole chapter contains hard-hitting truth. But it's a chapter that has helped me persevere through some very difficult times in my life. Otherwise, I may have given up all together.

I especially appreciate James 1:12:

"God blesses those who patiently endure testing and temptation. Afterward they will receive the crown of life that God has promised to those who love Him."

Earlier in James 1, in verse 3, we read that when our faith is tested, we gain endurance. Endurance is our first benefit of testing. As our endurance grows, we become mature, needing nothing. Maturity is our second benefit of testing. In verse 12, God blesses those who are patient - our third benefit. And our fourth benefit is our beautiful crown of life we will receive.

Knowing we are gaining something from the pain helps us to patiently endure the trials. The truth is that the trials will come no matter what our attitude. We can fuss, cuss and be angry. Or we can endure, asking God for grace and peace. I'll admit that I've done a little bit of both.

When we choose to be patient and keep our eyes on Jesus, the trials seem smaller and less scary. The trial may still be there, and we may still be suffering, but there is this unexplainable joy that comes. God's peace settles like a blanket over our hearts. We feel stronger and more powerful.

And we need that feeling. We need to know we can endure and that we are made strong through God's help. Imagine the alternative: a bunch of crybaby wimps that nobody wants to be around! Seriously, nobody wants to be wimpy or be friends with someone like that.

I personally prefer to spend most of my time with people who are patient and joyful in hard times. They empower me and make me feel that I can do anything. People like that are so encouraging! I want to be powerful and encouraging to others. I bet you do also. All of us want to be known as strong and helpful to others. When we are both strong and helpful, our lives feel full and complete.

And that's part of why we're here – to live full lives that give God glory and bless others. Remember that we will not always suffer. There will be a day when we move from this earthly realm into our heavenly home. All suffering, tears, pain, etc. will be gone and we will enjoy God's presence for the rest of forever. What a day that will be!

Day 322

Dry Bones, Hear the Word of the Lord

Ezekiel 37-38 / James 1:19-2:17 / Psalm 117 / Proverbs 28:1

I have been in church all my life. I was born into a family that attended the Methodist Church, where I was baptized as an infant (the Lord showed me that was my baby dedication). At the age of around 5, my parents received the baptism of the Holy Spirit with the evidence of speaking in tongues and began attending a charismatic church. That was New Covenant Church in Hampton, VA.

We moved to Tennessee in 1975 because my dad got a new job. The Lord called us into a small church that met in an old, beautiful house. My dad was the pastor of that church for about eight years. As far as a denomination, I don't remember what we called ourselves.

Following that, I have been involved with three other churches that were labeled either as charismatic or non-denominational. My husband and I are currently leading a house church. We are still not affiliated with any certain denomination.

I have watched the church be strong and I have watched her be weak. I've watched people in the church speak up for the weak, as well as ignore and even abuse the weak. I've seen healing, sickness, death, life and birth, radical moves of God, as well as quiet times of God's presence.

I've witnessed brothers and sisters in Christ fight and devour one another. I have been left wondering how anyone who names the name of Christ could do such things. Maybe it's not the doing; maybe it's the doing without repenting and making things right that I don't understand. It takes humility to admit one is wrong or has sinned against another person.

The current state of the church is a mixed bag. There is corruption, rampant sin, hidden sin, false teachers, false converts, and evil of every kind. But there is a remnant: those who are passionately in love with Jesus Christ and who want nothing more than to bring Him glory and to love and build others up.

I'm in the latter group. My heart for many years has been to see others as God created them and find ways to encourage them and help them be free. But even with this type of heart, there are times I have found myself weary of the apathy in the church, concerned for those who are asleep when they should be awake. Disappointed that the church is not rising to take places of authority across the earth as God mandated that we do.

However, I believe that all is not lost. I firmly believe God is preparing for Himself an army, a bride. He is coming back for a glorious church (Ephesians 5:27) that is strong on the earth and preparing to be married to her Bridegroom upon His return. As I read in Ezekiel 37 about Ezekiel's visit to the Valley of Dry Bones, my heart raced. I believe we are in such a season in the church. I believe God is calling out to the disconnected parts and commanding them to connect and become a body.

Why do I believe this? I'm watching as the church across all the earth awakens and prepares herself for battle and God's glory. Muscles and flesh are forming over the bones that have come together. Skin is forming to cover the bodies, and we are waiting for the breath of God to fill us so that we will arise as a strong army (Ezekiel 37:7-10). His breath is coming. Holy Spirit is on the move.

Are you prepared to receive His breath? Are you prepared to live again? Dry bones, hear the word of the Lord, "LIVE!"

Day 323

It's Time to Plant Seeds

Ezekiel 39:1-40:27 / James 2:18-3 / Psalm 118:1-18 / Proverbs 28:2

Have you ever looked up the meaning of your name? Or have you studied history to find people with your name to find out who they were and what they accomplished? When it comes to our names, not all of us have a biblical counterpart. Interestingly, when I look up Mary in the New Testament, which was first written in Greek, it means "Maria."

Hubby Jeff's name is not in the Bible, at least not literally. But I found a verse today that reminded me of his nature. The name Jeffrey means "peacemaker" and my hubby is a peacemaker, bridge builder, and one who generally knows how to diffuse a terrible situation. He walks in a lot of wisdom, gentleness, and respect.

The verse that reminded me of Jeff is James 3:18, and it says,

> "And those who are peacemakers
> will plant seeds of peace and
> reap a harvest of righteousness."

First, whatever we plant is what we will gather. The farming analogy of planting and harvesting is helpful here. If one plants bean seeds, he will harvest beans. If beets are planted, beets will be harvested, and so on. This scripture says that if one plants peace, they reap righteousness. Let's explore those two words to see how they relate to one another.

According to the Strong's Concordance, the word for "righteousness" in the verse above means in a broad sense, "state of him who is as he ought to be, righteousness, the condition acceptable to God. The doctrine concerning the way in which man may attain a state approved of God. Integrity, virtue, purity of life, rightness, correctness of thinking, feeling, and acting."

According to the Strong's Concordance, the word for "peace" means, "a state of national tranquility. Exemption from the rage and havoc of war. Peace between individuals, i.e. harmony, concord. Security, safety, prosperity, felicity, (because peace and harmony make and keep things safe and prosperous). Of the Messiah's peace: the way that leads to peace (salvation.) Of Christianity, the tranquil state of a soul assured of its salvation through Christ, and so fearing nothing from God and content with its earthly lot, of whatsoever sort that is. The blessed state of devout and upright men after death."

Yes, I gave you all the Strong's definitions for peace because they were all good! When we are made righteous through Jesus Christ, we are acceptable to and approved by God. We are only acceptable and approved because of Jesus Christ. Without Him, we would not be received. When we are made right with God, we have peace. Remember, the way that leads to peace is salvation.

It makes sense that if we are right with God (righteousness and peace) we would plant seeds of that right relationship. As we continue to plant what we've already received through Jesus Christ, we will continue to harvest the same. This is another way of saying that our faith in Jesus Christ causes us to do good works.

I'm reminded of another verse that goes along with what we're discussing. Romans 5:1, "Therefore, since we have been made right in God's sight by faith, we have peace with God because of what Jesus Christ our Lord has done for us."

If there is nothing but chaos in your life, you may need to consider whether you are in right-relationship with God. Foundationally, have you received Jesus Christ as Savior and Lord? After that, we stay right with God when we examine our hearts and repent from the sin that Holy Spirit shows us.

1 John 1:9 tells us,

> "But if we confess our sins to Him,
> he is faithful and just to forgive us our sins
> and to cleanse us from all wickedness."

It is possible, as well as fulfilling to one's soul, to maintain a right-relationship with God. We have already been given His peace and His righteousness, so let's continue to plant what we have been given.

185

Day 324

Can Jealousy be Positive?

Ezekiel 40:28-41:26 / James 4 / Psalm 118:19-29 / Proverbs 28:3-5

Many of us have struggled with jealousy. If you haven't, that's great! Jealousy and envy can cause us to want what someone else has. These are common sins, and most people deal with them at some level. Let's define jealousy and envy according to Merriam Webster.

Jealousy means, "feeling or showing an unhappy or angry desire to have what someone else has." Envy means, "the feeling of wanting to have what someone else has."

Scripture also talks about God being jealous for His people and the relationship He has with them. I'm going to share a verse with you and then we'll define God's jealousy to see how it compares with human jealousy.

James 4:5 says,

"Do you think the scriptures have no meaning?
They say that God is passionate that the Spirit He has placed within us should be faithful to Him."

The same verse in the NIV says it this way,

"Or do you think Scripture says without reason that He jealously longs for the Spirit He has caused to dwell in us?"

James 4:5, in the KJV reads:

"Do ye think that the scripture saith in vain,
The spirit that dwelleth in us lusteth to envy?"

The NIV translates the Greek word "phthonos" as "jealously." While the NLT uses the word "passionate" and the KJV uses "envy." Based on these simple definitions of the words jealously, passionate, and envy, it appears that both jealousy and envy may be used for either evil or good.

How so? How can a word that we have been taught is negative, be used in a positive sense? Word meanings shift when Holy Spirit gets involved. This will not apply to all words, but it does apply here.

When we surrendered to Jesus Christ, making Him Savior and Lord, we committed ourselves to Him fully. However, there is a process of total commitment that takes place over our entire lives. We are not able to give Him everything inside us all at once, i.e. all our attitudes, our past, our habits, our sin, etc. All these things have been covered by Jesus's sacrifice, but we must work to renew our minds, until we operate in accordance with what we've been given.

God knows that our surrendering and becoming holy is a process. Some of us readily submit everything to Him as we are made aware of it, and some of us are more reluctant. That reluctance may be because we don't want to see the true state of our hearts. Or it may be that once we've seen it, we are not prepared to change the way we think and act.

Our Father in heaven sees what sin does to us. He sees the pain sin causes; He sees the destruction and sorrow that are the result of sin. He wants us to be free because He loves us so much and it grieves Him to see us suffer. That is why He is jealous and envious that the Spirit within us would overtake our humanity. He wants us to be changed into His image so we can have more and more intimate fellowship with Him.

His death brought us life, and it also brought us an opportunity to live in love and community with God through His sacrifice. That's why God is jealous for you. He wants you to be free and He wants you all to Himself!

Day 325

Being in Community Brings Health

Ezekiel 42-43 / James 5 / Psalm 119:1-16 / Proverbs 28:6-7

Some churches practice laying on of hands, along with prayer, for various reasons. These prayers are for healing, encouragement, sending someone out on a short-term or long-term mission or endeavor, or releasing someone into a ministry. Apart from the fact that human touch is beneficial, what other benefit would there be in laying hands on someone?

I've had hands laid on me many times by those who have prayed; I've received love, warmth, encouragement, healing, and strength. Humans need physical contact with others. This need for physical contact begins at birth. Babies who are held, cuddled, rocked, and fed regularly thrive. Those who do not receive these things do not do well and some even die.

What about adults? Could adults who do not receive human touch also die? In some of the articles I read, contact with others can make your immune system strong, give you bodily strength, and may help avoid some cardiovascular diseases. So, from the youngest to the oldest, we must remember to embrace and affirm those we love. When we do, we are making them physically healthier!

James 5:13-16 leads us through a few scenarios of prayer. Here are those verses,

"Are any of you suffering hardships? You should pray. Are any of you happy? You should sing praises. Are any of you sick? You should call for the elders of the church to come and pray over you, anointing you with oil in the name of the Lord. Such a prayer offered in faith will heal the sick, and the Lord will make you well. And if you have committed any sins, you will be forgiven."

If one is suffering; she should pray. If one is happy, she should sing. If one is sick, she should ask for prayer. The prayer for the sick may include anointing with oil. And while this verse does not specifically mention the laying on of hands, that has been my experience. Sometimes during that prayer, God will speak over that person. Whether addressing their emotional and/or physical healing, or toward something that will give her strength.

We certainly need to be strengthened during these days on earth! Many are feeling the pressure of natural chaos as well as the spiritual battle all around us. This reminds me of another scripture that encourages us toward giving each other needed strength.

Hebrews 3:12-14 TPT says,

"So search your hearts every day, my brothers and sisters, and make sure that none of you has evil or unbelief hiding within you. For it will lead you astray and make you unresponsive to the living God. This is the time to encourage each other to never be stubborn or hardened by sin's deceitfulness. For we are mingled with the Messiah, if we will continue unshaken in this confident assurance from the beginning until the end."

We need to encourage each other. Yes, this is a need. If we fail to encourage our brothers and sisters in Christ, they may be suffering from sin, sickness, loneliness, as well as many other ills. We must be attentive to the needs of those close to us. No, we cannot meet all needs, but God will give us a group of family and friends with whom we can connect and for whom we can care.

If you are not part of a caring community of people who care for you; ones for whom you care, pray, hug, and lay hands on, please reach out today and get connected. Your life may depend upon it! Seriously, your immune system, your heart, and your well-being all depend on being in relationship with God and people that you trust.

Day 326

Yes, We Are All Priests

Ezekiel 44:1-45:12 / 1 Peter 1:1-12 / Psalm 119:17-32 / Proverbs 28:8-10

In reading about the priesthood, as the temple was restored in Ezekiel, a mixture of emotions was swirling around in my heart. When Ezekiel, who was born as one in line for the priesthood, but was serving as a prophet in Israel, describes these events, he is living with God's people in exile in Babylon. The temple described in this book is a temple that was experienced in a vision and was never built.

As God's people suffered in captivity, I'm sure they were tempted to give in to despair, but it was Ezekiel's job as a prophet to give them the word of the Lord and to encourage them that they had not been forgotten. God instructed Ezekiel to pay specific attention to the details of the heavenly vision of the temple and to instruct the people regarding what he saw.

Instead of writing about all the history and details of what happened in this vision, I want to explore what it means for us to be kings and priests to God today. Yes, there is a description of who a priest was, along with all his duties in the Old Covenant. However, now that we are in the New Covenant, what does it mean for us to operate as priests in God's Kingdom?

Let's begin with a few verses stating that we are priests.
1 Peter 2:5-9,

"And you are living stones that God is building into his spiritual temple. What's more, you are his holy priests. Through the mediation of Jesus Christ, you offer spiritual sacrifices that please God... you are a chosen people. You are royal priests, a holy nation, God's very own possession. As a result, you can show others the goodness of God, for he called you out of the darkness into his wonderful light."

Let's pull out two phrases to look at further. "You are His holy priests" and "you are royal priests." These two phrases are speaking to all of those who belong to God through Jesus Christ. All nationalities, along with both male and female are included in this priesthood. This is not a physical priesthood and not like either the ancient priesthood we read about in Israel or the current priesthood we see in some churches.

We no longer must wear all the priestly garments of linen; however, we do have a biblical counterpart in the white robes of salvation which the blood of Jesus bought for us as described in Revelation 19:7-8.

"Let us be glad and rejoice and let us give honor to him. For the time has come for the wedding feast of the Lamb, and his bride has prepared herself. She has been given the finest of pure white linen to wear. For the fine linen represents the good deeds of God's holy people."

We no longer must offer blood sacrifices to pay for our sin, for God made Christ, who never sinned, to be the offering for our sin, so that we could be made right with God through Christ. (2 Corinthians 5:21)

According to 1 Peter 1, we can offer spiritual sacrifices that please God. What are these spiritual sacrifices? Anything we freely offer to God would be considered a sacrifice – our praise, time, resources, or anything of value to us. When we choose to live a consecrated life, that is also a spiritual sacrifice. Any time we give up our will for His, we are offering God a sacrifice.

Spiritual sacrifices do not replace our relationship with God, rather they are born out of our love for Him as He pours His love on us. He does not demand the sacrifice, but it pleases Him. We do not offer sacrifices instead of spending time with Him; they are in addition.

Our priesthood is one in which we wear the white garments of salvation and offer back to God everything He has given us. I'm thankful to be this kind of priest; I'm thankful for the sacrifice on the cross of our High Priest Jesus Christ.

Day 327

The Humble are Easy to Teach

Ezekiel 45:13-46:24 / 1 Peter 1:13-2:10
Psalm 119:33-48 / Proverbs 28:11

Those who are humble and teachable are more successful than those who are not. As a mentor of others, my favorite type of person to walk alongside is the one who listens and acts upon what she or he hears. When I'm with a humble listener who does something with what we talk about, I can't wait to meet with that person again because I know they are going to be further along than when we last talked.

I have also met with those who want my input and opinion, but either they never got back with me, or I find out later that they did nothing with the wisdom that was shared with them. That always makes me sad for them because I realize they will not progress past that point until they act. If you want to be one who is always growing and changing, take counsel from others then do something with it.

As I read through the verses in Psalm 119 today, I noticed some direct requests from the Psalmist as He communicated with the Lord. Teach me – give me – direct me – turn my – fulfill Your – and take away. There was not a please in front of these requests which leads me to believe the writer (believed to be David, Ezra, or Daniel) was adamant on receiving what he was asking of God.

I also believe there was an expectation that the requests would be met with affirmation and results. What was the writer wanting to learn? Teach me Your ways - give me understanding - direct me in Your path - turn my heart toward Your statutes - turn my eyes away from worthless things - fulfill Your promises - take away disgrace.

Among this list were two that I would think the writer would be responsible to act upon; turn my heart and turn my eyes. Should we not turn our own heart and eyes? Yes, if we are speaking of our physical heart and eyes that would be true. However, I conclude that the writer was speaking of his spiritual heart and eyes and when speaking of spiritual things, Holy Spirit must be involved to create a shift.

I'm sure the writer understood after many years of seeking after God the difference between God's responsibility toward us and ours toward Him. There are requests we make of God and there are requests He makes of us. We must not be lazy Christians who expect no effort as we relate to God. He is more than willing to meet with us, and He will even initiate many of those meetings. However, He so enjoys when we initiate communication with Him.

There is also an indicator that the writer desires his heart and eyes be turned, meaning he is a willing participant in turning toward God's laws and away from worthless things. We can take action to turn toward God's law by reading our Bible and meditating on what we read. We can take action to turn away from worthless things by guarding what our eyes see (and what our ears hear). It takes hard work on our part to do both, but we will find ourselves rapidly growing in our faith when we make the effort.

When you are one who is willing both to turn toward and to turn away, you are a prime candidate for being taught, for growth, for maturity, and for a full, abundant, and beautiful life. You will have your pick of counselors, friends, and mentors. Your life will shine as an example to others. So, be teachable and be humble. You will never regret your choice.

Day 328

The Hard Work of Relationships

Ezekiel 47-48 / 1 Peter 2:11-3:7 / Psalm 119:49-64 / Proverbs 28:12-13

Relationships are what form our character and worldview. How we treat others proves our character and worldview. We learn more effectively when we can practice what we're learning with others. It does no good to read about concepts in books but never walk out those concepts.

Our first relationships are those in our home. First, the home in which we were raised, then the home in which we are adults and have our own families. Some of us are single, some are married, and some have children. The most foundational of relationships in our adult home begins with our spouse. It is this relationship that tests us, builds character, and shows to others either how we should or should not treat one another.

The Bible is helpful in teaching us how to treat one another and speaks about many different relational scenarios, from parents with their children, to bosses toward their workers. If you want to know how to treat others, you likely have an innate sense of that, but if you are unsure, the Word of God gives plenty of instruction.

1 Peter 3:1-7 speaks about the relationship between husbands and wives. Whether you are the husband or wife, be careful not to look only at how the other ought to be treating you. Look also at how you ought to be treating your spouse. Verse 1 tells wives to accept the authority of your husbands. In doing so, your godly lives will speak to them without any words.

Verse 7 tells husbands to give honor to their wives and treat them with understanding as you live together. Husbands are to treat their wives as equal partners. And they are to treat their wives with love so that their prayers will not be hindered.

There are benefits in wives treating husbands a certain way and in husbands treating wives a certain way. Wives be respectful and draw your husband into a relationship with Christ. In being honoring we are encouraging our husbands to submit to Jesus Christ. Husbands give honor to your wives so that your prayers will be answered.

What does it mean for a wife to accept the authority of her husband? The Strong's Concordance in one of the meanings of the word submit says, "to order under" or "to arrange under". This is a military term that is valuable in a family setting. When a wife arranges herself under her husband, she is partnering with him and being protected by him. Some see this role as demeaning, but it is not. It is a place for serving together, and a place of safety.

What does it mean for a husband to honor his wife? The Strong's Concordance says honor is "to value, reverence and count as precious." The husband is not the boss of the wife; he is partnering with her in a loving way. He sees her as his equal. And it's to his benefit to do this because as he honors his wife, the Lord will answer his prayers.

As the children see their parents treating one another with honor and love, they will feel safe and secure and will want to model this behavior toward others. No family does this perfectly but those who try will be richly rewarded for their hard work in treating others the way God desires.

If you are having relational problems in your life, check to be sure you are showing honor, love, and respect to those around you. Relationships are both difficult and rewarding but when done God's way, you will certainly find your life richer.

Day 329

The Condition of Our Hearts

Daniel 1:1-2:23 / 1 Peter 3:8-4:6 / Psalm 119:65-80 / Proverbs 28:14

Some of the sayings in the Bible are confusing, some are hard to understand, and some are just plain funny. Psalm 119:70 is such a funny verse. I want to give you a few translations so you can get an idea of what the meaning is.

> New Living Translation – "Their hearts are dull and stupid, but I delight in Your instruction."

> King James Version – "Their heart is as fat as grease; but I delight in Thy law."

> The Passion Translation – "Their hearts are dull and void of feelings, but I find my true treasure in your truth."

Before we move on to defining the meaning of this verse, I have a few observations. My first observation is that my "grandgirl" Heritage would not appreciate the word "stupid" because she has told me that is a mean word, and we are not supposed to say it. I remember when my sister's children were smaller that one of them came home from my parents' house telling her mother that Papa said the "s" word. Most of us would think of another forbidden word, but she was referring to the word "stupid."

As you may have guessed, this word has a long history of being a word we are not allowed to say in our family. My second observation is that having a heart "as fat as grease" is kind of gross to consider. As unappealing as that sounds, what does it mean? How does one's heart get into this condition?

The dull and stupid ones are referred to in verse 69 as "arrogant people who smear <the writer> with lies." The psalmist sounds a little bitter and angry and perhaps we would all feel the same way if someone was spreading lies about us. The psalmist also asserts that he is careful to follow God's ways, obeying His commandments. I can see why it would be offensive to have lies spread about you when you're doing your best to honor God.

Let's go back to how this dull, stupid, and greasy heart may have formed in the arrogant people. Here is a word picture I found in one commentary that describes a fat heart.

"As if he should say, my heart is a lean heart, a hungry heart, my soul loveth and rejoiceth in thy word. I have nothing else to fill it but thy word, and the comforts I have from it; but their hearts are fat hearts; fat with the world, fat with lust; they hate the word. As a full stomach loatheth meat and cannot digest it; so wicked men hate the word, it will not go down with them, it will not gratify their lusts." (William Fenner, cited in Spurgeon.)

A "fat heart" is filled with the things of the world and reminds me of 1 John 2:16 which says,

"For the world offers only a craving for physical pleasure, a craving for everything we see, and pride in our achievements and possessions. These are not from the Father but are from this world."

What about a lean heart? What about the heart that loves God's law? Psalm 119:97-99 tells us this,

"Oh, how I love your instructions! I think about them all day long. Your commands make me wiser than my enemies, for they are my constant guide. Yes, I have more insight than my teachers, for I am always thinking of your laws."

The choice is ours. We may choose a fat, lazy, greasy heart or we may choose a lean, attentive, hungry heart. I have chosen the latter and have made that choice for many years. I pray you are doing the same!

Day 330

Things That Stand in Heaven

Daniel 2:24-3:30 / 1 Peter 4:7-5:14
Psalm 119:81-96 / Proverbs 28:15-16

When people speak, we either believe what they say or doubt the validity of what they are sharing. Some speakers are credible, and some are not. The credible are likely those we know personally or those who have been recommended to us. We may also believe their words because what they are speaking about is familiar to us.

On the other hand, there may be times we do not know and trust the speaker. Perhaps they have a poor reputation or maybe we don't know them at all. Or maybe the things they are sharing are things we've studied and disproved for ourselves. Some go into conversations with an open heart, and some go in suspiciously. I believe it's wise to go in with an open heart, but to guard what you place into your foundational belief system.

I prefer to be known as a woman of her word. Lying is something I can't tolerate. As a matter of fact, when one of my children was young (I will withhold the name to protect the reformed) this child told lies on a regular basis. I finally got so tired of the lying that I threatened with this, "God is going to tell me every time you lie!" I walked out of that room praying for God to back me up. And He did! This child is now an adult who loves truth, so we both tell this story from time to time and just laugh. A lot has changed!

When we're unsure whether to believe what we're hearing, we can at least be certain there is One whose word is always the truth.

That being true, we can hold the things we hear in comparison to His words to determine if what we're hearing is factual.

Here is the verse that caught my attention from today's reading. Psalm 119:89,

> "Your eternal word, O LORD,
> stands firm in heaven."

If you have studied much scripture, you know that sometimes Jesus Christ is referred to as the Word, or the Logos. This is not the same Hebrew word here. The word used here means "speech, words, or utterance." So, this verse refers to the words of a person and not the person Himself.

However, if God has spoken something, we can be assured it is truth. If He says He will do something, He will. If He says He is a certain way, be assured it is true. If God has said it, you can confidently put your trust in what you heard. The next question is, "How do we hear God speak?"

We hear Him through the Bible, which is His written Word. We hear Him through His voice speaking to our hearts. We hear Him in dreams and visions. We hear Him when others speak the truth. If what you're hearing seems contrary to the truth you've come to trust, it's time to do some research.

I encourage you not to take everything you hear as truth. There are times you will hear full truth, times you'll hear partial truth, and times you'll hear a total fabrication. We must learn to discern the difference. Many false religions have begun because lies were mixed with truth and gullible people believed what they heard instead of studying to confirm.

I'm not being disrespectful in calling some gullible. Some are ignorant or uninformed and some believe everything they hear. That is not wise. If something doesn't sit well with you, ask someone for facts to back up the claims. Study God's Word, ask a Bible teacher you trust for help, or whatever you must do to settle your heart only on truth.

As a final authority, always check what you're hearing with scripture. If you don't understand what you're reading, ask for help. There is no shame in asking someone to assist you in interpreting what you're hearing, and you may go away much wiser.

Day 331

Eight Steps to Building

Daniel 4 / 2 Peter 1 / Psalm 119:97-112 / Proverbs 28:17-18

"Work hard and keep your nose clean" is a saying that not many these days may understand. I haven't heard it spoken in a while, but I found some information on the origin of this phrase. And no, this doesn't mean to use a tissue or handkerchief to wipe one's nose.

This phrase originated from another phrase which is "keep the hands clean," which was widely used in England in the 18th century. The phrase meant to avoid corruption and when it became adopted in the US, it became modified to "keep your nose clean," which literally meant to keep your nose out of what doesn't concern you. This new phrase then became widely adopted to mean avoiding doing anything shady. (Source: theidioms.com)

When one is working hard, she usually has no time for getting into trouble because there is simply too much work to do. Most think of work in terms of vocation or schooling, but we also have spiritual work to do. We've talked before about the fact that our faith is proven by our works (James 2:26). Let's see what other work we are to do considering what God has provided for us.

2 Peter 1:5 says,

> "In view of all this, make every effort
> to respond to God's promises."

In view of what? Verse 3 tells us that God has given us everything we need for living a godly life, and we received all of this by coming to know Him. Because God has given us everything through Jesus Christ, we have a responsibility. We don't just receive God's gift and do nothing with it; that would be the same as burying our gifts and talents and not allowing them to grow. What are the things we are to do?

We have received faith, and we are to add moral excellence to our faith. To our moral excellence we are to add knowledge, to knowledge, self-control. To our self-control we must add patient endurance; to endurance we must add godliness. To our godliness we must add brotherly affection, and the last thing these verses tell us to add is love for everyone.

This may sound either like a math problem or a construction project. Depending upon which way your brain works, either would be appropriate. Since my husband is a contractor, I prefer to think of faith as the foundation upon which moral excellence is built. The layers after that are added as each previous layer becomes firm and stable.

Or, if you're a foodie, you might like to see these eight layers as a banana split! Faith is the banana and love for everyone would be the cherry on top. The other six attributes are the ice-cream and toppings.

I'm not saying one must add moral excellence before knowledge, but I also wonder if the writer had a certain process in mind, knowing that each layer would be a firm foundation for the next. Some may work toward one attribute at a time, and some may work on all eight positive traits a little each day until they are mastered.

However you choose to work on these eight disciplines, I believe the more important topic is to be aware of them and add them to your heart and life. I can imagine that one could spend all her life on these eight and will have built a great reputation with others, as well as having been pleasing to God.

Where will you start to build upon your faith? Yes, I do believe faith must be the foundation because it is by faith we received Jesus Christ, and it is by faith we continue. I encourage you to begin or continue building today!

Day 332

What Controls You?

Daniel 5 / 2 Peter 2 / Psalm 119:113-128 / Proverbs 28:19-20

Several years ago, when my children were small, the Lord talked to me about giving up two things. He asked me to give them up because they had control over me instead of me having control over them. I will tell you about both things, then I want to share a verse from today's reading.

The first thing the Lord asked me to give up was watching Star Trek and all the subsequent series. Why? When my children were small, I was concerned they would be afraid of the alien images on the show, so I would only watch when they were asleep. All three of them have prophetic giftings so all three were known to be negatively affected by certain images, especially on television.

I remember Matthew, my oldest, running out of the room when something that scared him appeared on the screen. I thought I was fine to watch the shows when the children couldn't see them, but this is what God said to me. "Maria, if your children do not need to be watching them because it is affecting them prophetically, you do not need to watch them either."

So, for many years I did not watch anything associated with Star Trek. It was probably about fifteen to twenty years that I took this Star Trek fast. I have only in recent years caught up with what I missed and enjoyed. I was pleased to discover I was no longer ruled by having to watch the shows.

The second thing the Lord asked me to give up was drinking Dr. Pepper. There was something unique about the flavor of that drink that I could not get enough of. Again, the Lord alerted me to the fact that I was being controlled by something, and He asked me to stop drinking it. I never went back to drinking it.

I tried Diet Dr. Pepper many years later but found I had no interest. Now, I wouldn't drink any sodas because they are so harmful due to the corn syrups and heavy sugars. My current clean eating lifestyle does not allow me to pollute my body with this or any other processed foods.

The verse that has me remembering these stories is found in 1 Peter 2:19,

"They promise freedom, but they themselves are slaves of sin and corruption. For you are a slave to whatever controls you. Those who are promising freedom are the false teachers who lead others astray and into sin."

The phrase that struck me most was the fact that I become a slave to anything that controls me. That is eye-opening and I believe we must operate in discernment, so we don't become trapped by anything. We must be controlled only by Holy Spirit. I know God will faithfully show us if there are any areas where we are being controlled by sin. Are you brave enough to ask Him to open your eyes to those areas?

I pray you make the choice to ask this question of God. Asking the question need not be a fearful task because God only wants to bring freedom to our souls. It may be hard to give up that thing or habit, but in the end, you will be so glad you did because you will feel free and light. Most of the time we're not aware we are being controlled, but once we've tasted freedom there is something in us that never wants to return to the chains!

$\mathcal{D}$ay 333

Are You Vulnerable to Deception?

Daniel 6 / 2 Peter 3 / Psalm 119:129-152 / Proverbs 28:21-22

Have you ever known someone who was so gullible they believed anything anyone told them? Whether it was true or not? Or maybe you've been the gullible one. Some of us are suspicious of everyone and some of us believe the best of everyone. Then some are somewhere in the middle in the system of gullibility.

I believe I fall in the middle. I tend to want to believe that others would not lie to me or deceive me. But I've been around long enough to know that people not only lie, but they also paint a picture of themselves as better than they are because of their insecurity. There is also the possibility that someone has told a lie long enough that they begin to believe the lies are the truth.

When leading others, it's important to rely on God's wisdom for discernment in all situations. It's easy to be fooled or get sucked into a trap of deception. It can be especially difficult when listening to two sides of a story because you want to fully believe each side. Most of the time, if not all the time, the truth of a situation lies somewhere between the two stories. That's why it's important to listen to Holy Spirit.

In reading Daniel 6 today, I started wondering what made king Darius agree to listen to the plan of the administrators and satraps. The leaders knew they were trying to trap Daniel, but King Darius didn't know that. Maybe Darius was excited to be worshipped, since that was the proposal. Could it be that he was so self-centered that he believed his leaders simply wanted him to receive worship for thirty days?

It's possible. I can think of no other reason Darius would agree to this plan. I wonder also if Darius immediately suspected his leaders of betrayal once they came to him with the accusation against Daniel. Or did it take him some time to figure that out?

Being in leadership can be rewarding and difficult. It's rewarding because we are allowed to assist others. It can be difficult because there will always be those who will betray or deceive us, whether intentionally or not.

We must always walk in forgiveness, or we will become cynical and bitter toward those we're trying to help. I don't think Darius was in a forgiving mood when he discovered he had been deceived. His solution was to subject the deceivers to the same punishment they had tried to perpetrate on Daniel. It was certainly a gruesome ending.

There may be times you would like to throw your enemy to the lions, but then you would go to jail - that is if we even had man-eating lion pits today. But how do we treat those who have deceived us? We are certainly more cautious with those people, as well as with others going forward. One thing we must guard against is being suspicious of everyone we meet. We must still believe others are innocent until proven otherwise.

This reminds me of a verse in 1 Corinthians 13:7 in the Amplified Bible,

"Love bears all things (regardless of what comes),
believes all things (looking for the best in each one),
hopes all things (remaining steadfast during difficult times),
endures all things (without weakening.)"

Did you see that phrase: "Looking for the best in each one."? We must do that. If God has brought someone into our lives, then we must honor God by looking for His Spirit deposited within that person. I assure you it's there. We may immediately see only the trauma and the drama, but once that person is loved and healed, God wants to use them to further His Kingdom on the earth.

Take the time to look for that Kingdom purpose in others. If you find none, you may have some "tricky advisors" on your hands, and it may be time to send them packing! Discern and learn.

Day 334

A Shiny New Soul

Daniel 7 / 1 John 1 / Psalm 119:153-176 / Proverbs 28:23-24

I've been pondering the difficulty of being open and honest with others. I'm not saying it's difficult to be truthful and not to lie; I'm talking about being willing to be vulnerable. It's a scary thought for another human to know who we are deep on the inside. Sometimes we don't even know the depths of what hides in our hearts; only God knows that darkness.

Even those of us who try to live a life that pleases God are painfully aware of our shortcomings. All of us have areas where we miss it, blow it, or honestly sin according to scripture. Lying, cheating, stealing, anger, and many other things can lie hidden in our hearts without us being fully aware. Yes, even little white lies are sins. Usually, anything we do to protect ourselves and to hide from others gets us into trouble.

What if we lived in a world where everyone lived honestly? That sounds like a great idea until we consider that we cannot fathom the things we would hear and know about those around us. If the honesty of others was toward positive traits, that would be great, but if we had to hear about the evil in the hearts of others it would be overwhelming.

There is One who sees every piece of our hearts, even the ones of which we are unaware, and He loves us perfectly despite our weaknesses. He sees that we lie to make ourselves look better to others. He sees that we cheat on our taxes, or that we secretly hate others. He sees that we avoid our responsibilities because we are either too lazy or too tired.

What if we began by being willing to be honest with God? He won't reject us. As a matter of fact, we will receive forgiveness and healing for the terrible things hidden in our hearts. As usual, I have a few verses that have sparked my thinking in this direction.

"If we claim we have no sin, we are only fooling ourselves and not living in the truth. But if we confess our sins to him, he is faithful and just to forgive us our sins and to cleanse us from all wickedness. If we claim we have not sinned, we are calling God a liar and showing that his word has no place in our hearts." — 1 John 1:8-10

These three verses, using very direct speech, may seem harsh or scary to us. But if we accept them as truth, there is freedom hidden in these words. What would it look like to live in the truth? What would it feel like to have our sins forgiven? What would it feel like to be cleansed from all wickedness?

I guess it would be a little like going through a car wash for the soul. We would all be squeaky and shiny! I want that! I'm sure you're thinking to yourself that this sounds great, that is until the next day when you stumble into sin yet again. What then? Rinse and repeat and become that shiny new person all over again.

Even if we must come to God daily (which we should) to ask Him to search our hearts to find the areas of sin, I believe it is worth the effort so that we can live feeling guilt-free. We can't shock or surprise God with our thoughts and actions. He experienced all our sins on the cross and He gave His life to pay the cost of what we have done and will do.

Let's simply receive that payment as a gift and ask God to daily put us through that car wash of the soul!

Day 335

Be The Love

Daniel 8 / 1 John 2:1-17 / Psalm 120 / Proverbs 28:25-26

All of us look for those to emulate, those we can admire, those we can even call heroes. We are all wired to look outside ourselves for greatness, hoping we can also be better people. No one wants to be evil unless they are deceived by the devil. Most of us want to improve, grow, and mature.

So, how do we find the right role model? Who should we look to as an example of how to live? There is nothing wrong with admiring those who have worked hard and are living with honesty and integrity. Those who are living this way should be prepared to be watched and to have others wish to pattern their lives after them. That is both humbling and sobering.

While we may look to others who are mature and living life with integrity, there is another we should also look to, so we know how to live. When Jesus came to earth as a man, He was God in the flesh. He lived with the same joys and sorrows we did, only He lived without sin. Jesus also showed us, by His example, what the Father is like.

Here is our portion of scripture for today's thoughts. It is from 1 John 2:7-11.

"Dear friends, I am not writing a new commandment for you; rather it is an old one you have had from the very beginning. This old commandment—to love one another—is the same message you heard before. Yet it is also new. Jesus lived the truth of this commandment, and you also are living it. For the darkness is disappearing, and the true light is already shining. If anyone claims, 'I am living in the light,' but hates a fellow believer, that person is still living in darkness. Anyone who loves a fellow believer is living in the light and does not cause others to stumble. But anyone who hates a fellow believer is still living and walking in darkness. Such a person does not know the way to go, having been blinded by the darkness."

I'm noticing something about the book of 1 John; it is very direct in presenting the truth. If you have been reading the book along with my devotionals, you already have probably had your toes stepped on a few times. I know I have. Jesus lived according to the commandment to love one another. And we must do the same.

If we hate a fellow follower of Jesus, we are deceived and living in darkness. I think each of us should take a few minutes and ask God if we are living in light and love, or if we have some forgiving to do. I hope you take the time to check your heart. I certainly have.

Jesus looked past the sins and shortcomings of others, realizing they needed an encounter with love and truth. Jesus was both love and truth. He brought that needed encounter to everyone who would receive Him.

We must do the same. We must be willing to look past the trauma and the drama and love someone the way Jesus loves them. Sometimes that requires a lot of patience. Not everyone gets it quickly so we must be prepared to walk with others until they can hear the truth. Truth is heard when love is present. Be willing to be the love of Jesus to those God brings to you.

Day 336

We Live between Two Kingdoms

Daniel 9-11:1 / 1 John 2:18-3:6 / Psalm 121 / Proverbs 28:27-28

We live between two kingdoms: the kingdom of light and the kingdom of darkness. Not only do we live between these two kingdoms, but people are also divided. They must choose to live under one kingdom or the other. There is the Jesus Christ Kingdom and there is the anti-Jesus Christ kingdom. Under which kingdom do you live?

As followers of Jesus, we are exhorted in scripture to live in the world but not of the world. In 1 John 2:15 we read,

> "Do not love this world nor the things
> it offers you, for when you love the world,
> you do not have the love of the Father in you."

This is one of several verses that contrast living in the world, versus living of the world.

Our perspective, our rules, our weapons, along with everything else we've been given as citizens of Heaven are very different from the things available to those who belong to the system of the world and the devil. One kingdom is fueled by love, the other by fear. One is fueled by building up, the other by tearing down.

My belief is that no one would willingly choose the kingdom of hatred and tearing down if they had the spiritual eyes to see truth. If everyone saw the beauty of truth, they would choose that path every time. Therefore, we must work to open the eyes of those who are blinded by the ruler of this world (the devil). But how do we do that?

We must first know who we are according to the Spirit.

226

1 John 2:20-21 says this:

"But you are not like that, for the Holy One has given you his Spirit, and all of you know the truth. So, I am writing to you not because you don't know the truth but because you know the difference between truth and lies."

We help others see the kingdom of love through our knowledge of truth and through prayer! We are the keepers of truth. But we must not keep the truth to ourselves. Truth is meant to be shared with others for the sake of their freedom. When we have received freedom as the people of God, our hearts are moved to share that freedom with those who don't know.

We are in a spiritual war, one that has lasted for centuries. This war began when the serpent deceived Eve and enticed her into eating the fruit God had forbidden her to eat. That day the enemy declared war on those loved of God. And that day God began a plan to win us back to His heart and to give us our freedom again.

God is not content for us to live in darkness; that's why He sent His Son Jesus Christ.

"For once you were full of darkness, but now you have light from the Lord. So, live as people of light! For this light within you produces only what is good and right and true." —Ephesians 5:8-9

Those of us in Christ are no longer part of the dark kingdom; we are part of the kingdom of light, and we are lighting the way for others to see and receive what we have been given.

Day 337

Go Agape Someone

Daniel 11:2-35 / 1 John 3:7-24 / Psalm 122 / Proverbs 29:1

Have you ever thought about whether you would give your life for someone else if that was required? It's a sobering thought. We know Jesus Christ gave His life for ours. Maybe you've considered that you would be willing to die if it saved someone you loved. Maybe you're not sure how you would respond if you met with this type of choice; I can certainly understand that!

1 John 3:16 says this,

> "We know what real love is
> because Jesus gave up His life for us.
> So, we also ought to give up our lives
> for our brothers and sisters."

Does this verse mean that if we really love someone, we must die for them? That sounds a little too much like Romeo and Juliet to me. I'm not sure I'm ready to die for my fellow believers.

Thankfully, we are not required to physically die for others; Jesus already accomplished what was needed in that area. His death brought our forgiveness. We give up our lives to love others in different ways. We give up our time, resources, and heart space so that others may become free and grow in Christ.

Part of the confusion with the above scripture is the definition of love. There are four words for love in the Bible. Those words are "eros", "storge", "philia", and "agape."

"Eros" is defined as "physical, sensual intimacy between a husband and wife."

"Storge," (pronounced STO-ree), is defined as "cherishing one's kindred, especially parents or children."

"Philia" is defined as "close friendship or brotherly love."

"Agape" is defined as "pure, willful, sacrificial love, that intentionally desires another's highest good."

It is agape love that we are referring to today. Jesus loved us this way and we are to love others this way. We are often taught to look out for number one by society. But that is the opposite of what Jesus taught. If we are fully loved by God (and we are) we are free to love others unselfishly because we won't fear that our needs won't be met.

When our needs are met through Holy Spirit, we are excited to love others with agape love. When our souls are healthy, we don't fear loving others; either because we might be rejected, or because we might wear ourselves out. Give what you have and stop when you feel you need a break.

I caution against giving without stopping because that will exhaust your resources. Give according to Holy Spirit's leading. And rest from giving according to His leading. One cannot give everything to everyone, but we may give what we can to the ones God highlights to us. That is enough and God will be pleased.

Many times, if we encounter someone who is over-giving it is often because she or he is struggling with self-worth. Our giving does not make us worthy, but it does make us obedient. That is all God is asking for, obedience. That pleases Him and we are blessed in the giving.

Ask God today who you can love. And what loving action He would like for you to do to affirm that action. You will be blessed; the person will be blessed, and God will be smiling!

Day 338

Take a Chance

Daniel 11:36-12:13 / 1 John 4 / Psalm 123 / Proverbs 29:2-4

There are times when I don't feel loved, or even when I simply don't love myself. Just because we don't feel like we are loved doesn't mean we are not. Sometimes our feelings lie to us. There are times when someone else shares a positive perspective they have of me with me. I'm usually both encouraged and amazed. Not many are aware of the positive impact they have on others.

Why do you suppose that is? Why aren't we aware of the blessing we are to others? One, we may be giving to the world from who we are naturally and not be aware of the blessing we bring. Or two, we may have poor self-worth. And, consequently, have no idea of how we encourage those around us. I believe we can work toward not only being aware but also intentional in allowing our unique expression to be felt in the world.

Our basis of love as followers of Jesus Christ is found in 1 John 4:9-10a which reads,

> "God showed how much He loved us
> by sending His one and only Son into the world
> so that we might have eternal life through Him.
> This is real love..."

I appreciate that last phrase, "This is real love." We talked yesterday about the agape love of God, a love that pours itself out for the good of others. The Father through His Son Jesus did that for us already. Now, we must become aware of the love already given. To become aware, we must be informed and have our hearts opened by Holy Spirit to receive this love.

As sometimes happens, I'm remembering the lyrics to the worship song, "Reckless Love," by Cory Asbury. I want to share a portion of those lyrics with you.

> Oh, the overwhelming, never-ending,
> reckless love of God
>
> Oh, it chases me down,
> fights 'til I'm found,
> leaves the 99
>
> And I couldn't earn it,
> and I don't deserve it, still, Y
> ou give Yourself away
>
> Oh, the overwhelming, never-ending,
> reckless love of God

Please hear me: the love of God exists, period. Not only does His love exist, but it is also available for you and me. His love is free. His love is accessible. His love brings strength, courage, warmth, and many other things into our souls.

Imagine His love was sitting on a table in your kitchen. You walk up to the table and see the love there. Then you reach your hand out, pick the love up and place it into your chest.

Maybe that sounds far-fetched, but I invite you to imagine

yourself doing just that. Pick up His freely available love and take it into yourself. Then see if your perspective on life changes. I believe it will! The circumstances may not change but you will change. You will begin to believe you can do things you did not believe you could.

You will believe that you are valuable, wanted, and loved! You will believe you have something to offer to those around you. You will notice creative ideas coming to mind and you will have a burning desire to follow through on that creativity.

Now that you've read this entry, you have two options. You can walk away and forget what you heard Holy Spirit say to you through these words. Or you can act, and I have a feeling Holy Spirit is giving you an action step as you read. Do it! Take a chance, be daring, step out and watch your life be crazy blessed!

Day 339

The Safety of Staying Away

Hosea 1-3 / 1 John 5 / Psalm 124 / Proverbs 29:5-8

When you were little, your parents taught you to stay away from anything that would hurt you. You were taught not to touch the stove eye because you would be burned. When you were young, you were taught to look both ways before crossing the street, preferably still holding your parents' hands.

Now that I have grandbabies, I'm doing all this reinforcing again. Warnings are given, hands are reached for, and when necessary little ones are moved out of the way. But at some point, we mature, and we learn to self-govern. If we learn self-governing well when we are little, it is not a difficult transition.

Sometimes, when we grow up, we are challenged. No one is watching over us any longer to make sure we are safe and out of trouble. At least, we don't see that someone is watching.

God is always watching, not because He can't wait to rap us on our knuckles, but because He knows the dangers that wait if we make poor choices. He loves us. It makes Him sad to see us walk into danger.

1 John 5:21 says this,

> "Dear children, keep away from anything
> that might take God's place in your hearts."

You may first be thinking that this warning presents no danger and wondering why it would be included with thoughts on keeping away from danger. There is danger in allowing other things to take God's place in our hearts, and it is varied.

For example, we will not hear God's warning voice if He is not first in our hearts because other loves and voices will have crowded Him out. Another danger is that we will see God from a skewed perspective depending upon what has taken His place in our affections. Consider that as Jesus-followers our lives are meant to belong to Him. He should have our love, our attention, our focus as we work, etc. If He is not in charge of all that we are, our lives will suffer in that we will not fully fulfill the plans He has placed within us.

Of course, we will not see or do all He planned because we are finite humans, but wouldn't it be an exciting adventure to work hard to always hear Him and follow that path He has planned for us? Sometimes we believe we want our own way. But once we realize true joy is found in following the way He leads, there is more than enough adventure, joy, love, and mystery when we stay on His path. Not to mention we will also experience the safety of staying in His will.

Day 340

Go in Strength and Power

Hosea 4-5 / 2 John / Psalm 125 / Proverbs 29:9-11

As I've read the Bible these past 50+ years, I've developed some favorite verses and even some whole chapters that I really enjoy reading again and again. I very much enjoy reading Romans 8 and how we can never be separated from the love of God. I gain confidence by reading Hebrews 11 and remembering how my spiritual ancestors stood strong in their faith. I could name many other verses and chapters.

The truth is, I've come to love the Word of God in a very real and deep way. God's word, both written and spoken, are life to me and a strong foundation upon which I stand. I can't imagine being in the company of those who do not have access to a Bible either physically or online. It is still forbidden in some countries to own this important book. That tells me that the enemy spirits in those places are fearful of others knowing this living truth.

When God's Word is hidden in our hearts, we are less likely to be trapped by sin. Psalm 119:11 TPT says,

> "I consider your Word to be my greatest treasure,
> and I treasure it in my heart to keep me
> from committing sin's treason against you."

God's Word is not simply written on a page for us to read; it is alive. Hebrews 4:12 TPT reads,

"For we have the living Word of God, which is full of energy, like a two-mouthed sword. It will even penetrate to the very core of our being where soul and spirit, bone and marrow meet! It interprets and reveals the true thoughts and secret motives of our hearts."

These verses shouldn't scare us away; they give us strength and put courage into us. There is a chapter from today's reading that makes me feel strong and powerful. I want to include that entire short chapter for you to read.

Psalm 125 TPT reads,

"Those who trust in the Lord are as unshakable, as unmovable as mighty Mount Zion! Just as the mountains surround Jerusalem, so the Lord's wraparound presence surrounds his people, protecting them now and forever. The wicked will not always rule over the godly, provoking them to do what is evil. God, let your goodness be given away to your good people, to all your righteous ones! But those who turn away from truth—them you will turn away from you, to follow their crooked ways. You will give them just what they deserve. May Israel experience peace and prosperity!"

Do you see what I mean? This short chapter makes us want to stand taller without fear. When we trust in the Lord, we are un-shakable. We are as strong and unmovable as Mount Zion, which has never moved. The Lord surrounds His people – all of us – in the same way that there are mountains that surround the city of Jerusalem. Now we have a beautiful word picture, and we can imagine the Lord camping all around us.

Have you ever imagined the Lord near you? He is always nearby. He always surrounds us. Hebrews 13:5 TPT says this,

"Don't be obsessed with money but live content with what you have, for you always have God's presence. For hasn't he promised you, 'I will never leave you, never! And I will not loosen my grip on your life!'"

We always have God's presence. He will never leave us. He will never loosen His grip on our lives. Go in the strength of those words and have a powerful week!

Day 341

Be A Joyful Giver

Hosea 6-9 / 3 John / Psalm 126 / Proverbs 29:12-14

Now that we have entered the Christmas season, part of the joy of the holidays is that we are blessed to experience the heart and act of giving. As we celebrate the birth of Jesus Christ, by far the greatest gift given to us by the Father, we are all reminded about the generosity God has shown us. When we experience generosity, most of us are compelled to also be generous.

The Father initiated giving and He knows that His heart to give and bless will spur us to do the same. We have been given so much, the first of which is natural life. We were created in the image of God and given the breath of life. Whether our lives are filled with blessing or difficulty, most of us have much for which to be thankful.

Out of the abundance of what we've been given, most want to find a way to give to and bless others, especially at this time of year. Many are looking for ways to give to those less fortunate and that is a worthy act that I highly encourage everyone to engage in. We could find and quote scripture after scripture on generosity, giving, etc. I want to look at one set of verses for today.

"Dear friend, you are being faithful to God when you care for the traveling teachers who pass through, even though they are strangers to you. They have told the church here of your loving friendship. Please continue providing for such teachers in a manner that pleases God. For they are traveling for the Lord, and they accept nothing from people who are not believers. So, we ourselves should support them so that we can be their partners as they teach the truth." — 3 John 5-8

242

It's easy to give to our family and friends but what about when we are asked to give to strangers, or even to someone who we consider to be an enemy? In the season of giving, I'm excited to give gifts to my family and friends. When given an opportunity, I also enjoy giving to strangers. However, what would I do if I found out my enemy had a need? Would I cheerfully give gifts to her?

2 Corinthians 9:7 says,

"You must each decide in your heart how much to give. And don't give reluctantly or in response to pressure. 'For God loves a person who gives cheerfully.'"

What does it mean to give cheerfully? The Greek word from the Strong's Concordance means "joyous, merry, prompt, willing and hilarious." When I read these descriptive words, I think of a person who can't wait to give. A person who says "yes" even before giving the idea full thought. A person who is so happy to give that they are giddy.

How many of us feel this way when giving? I'd say there are times when we know we should give so we give but our hearts are irritated that we must give. How many times have you celebrated that you had an opportunity to give?

Jeff and I were recently eating with a friend who shared with us a story of another friend who had been given an opportunity to give. Do you know what her response was? She joyfully gave thanks for being thought of and for the opportunity to give. If all of us saw the blessings that were activated and released in the Spirit when we gave, we would joyfully do so more often!

Day 342

No Is a Complete Sentence

Hosea 10-14 / Jude / Psalm 127 / Proverbs 29:15-17

In college I took classes that would have helped me had I chosen a career in construction. I took drafting classes, an intro to computer aided drafting, cost estimation for construction, a shop class, and several other classes. I didn't end up in the construction field, although I worked for a construction company first as their draftsperson, then as the front office person.

So, it was interesting when God led my husband in 2000 to become a residential contractor. As I read through scripture, I've noticed several verses that speak about building. I read a couple of verses today that caught my eye from this perspective.

Psalm 127:1-2 reads,

"Unless the LORD builds a house, the work of the builders is wasted. Unless the LORD protects a city, guarding it with sentries will do no good. It is useless for you to work so hard from early morning until late at night, anxiously working for food to eat; for God gives rest to His loved ones."

One truth in these two verses is that if we are not led by God to engage in our work, we will not have a full measure of success. Sure, we will probably do well, accomplish tasks, and make money to feed our families. But I can't help but believe there will be a greater measure of the blessing of God if we have followed Him into our chosen profession.

We may find ourselves working harder instead of smarter. We may experience many setbacks instead of a flow of blessing and fulfillment. Every job will of course have difficulty but when we are operating in that place of grace it is very different to operating from a place of striving in our own strength.

There is a certain rest and peace present when we're walking where God has equipped and called us. That brings our thoughts to the second idea I want to highlight in the verses above. When we are walking where God has called us, there is rest in our work. Rest does not mean we are constantly sitting with our feet up or sleeping, allowing everyone else to do all the work. Rest is a state of our souls.

Rest for the soul comes when we allow God to carry our burdens instead of carrying them ourselves. The word rest in the verse above does also refer to sleep. The meaning is that if we have given our troubles and worries to God, we will be able to rest and to sleep without being concerned about the things happening around us.

If your job, family, friends, or life situations are keeping you awake at night, it's time for an evaluation. Maybe there is an area where you are involved, and God does not want you there. Or maybe you are taking on the weight of another person or situation. Be careful to do neither of these, but to give them to God in prayer. When it comes to our own burdens and troubles, it is a little harder because we feel responsible for these people, things, and situations.

We can certainly be responsible without carrying the mental and emotional load. God's shoulders are strong and broad enough to carry this load; ours are not. God does not expect us to wear ourselves out in any situation. I believe that if we are submitting everything to

Him in prayer and giving everything our best efforts, God is pleased and that is enough.

You've probably heard the saying that. "No is a complete sentence." It is okay to put things off, admit you are not able to do certain things, and to say "no." We are humans not superhumans!

Do your best, honor God and love people.

That is enough.

# Day 343

Joyful Blessings

Joel 1-3 / Revelation 1 / Psalm 128 / Proverbs 29:18

"Joyful, joyful we adore Thee
God of glory, Lord of love
Hearts unfold like flowers before thee
Opening to the sun above
Melt the clouds of sin and sadness,
Drive the dark of doubt away,
Giver of immortal gladness,
Fill us with the light of day."
— *Hymm written by Henry van Dyke in 1907,*
to be sung to Beethoven's "Ode to Joy"

Sometimes nothing expresses one's worship quite like a hymn. They are doctrinally sound; the tune is usually simple to follow, and the words will bring just the right strength we need. I thought of the above verse to the song "Joyful, Joyful We Adore Thee" when I read Psalm 128.

Psalm 128:1-2 reads,

"How joyful are those who fear the LORD,
all who follow His ways! You will enjoy the fruit of your labor.
How joyful and prosperous you will be!"

Reading those two verses made me smile, and gave me great hope for the present, and for the future. I want to look at the fullness of a few words in these verses because I have a feeling there is a rich blessing underneath. As usual, I will use the Strong's Concordance to find the Hebrew meaning of the following words:

"Joyful" means "happy or blessed."

"Fear" means "fearing; morally reverent; afraid, fearful."

"Fruit of labor" means "product, produce, acquired property (as a result of work.)"

"Prosperous" means "good, pleasant, agreeable (to the senses), excellent, rich, valuable in estimation, good understanding, kind, and bounty (among other things.)"

The key to these joyful blessings is the fear of the Lord. We are not to be afraid of the Lord, but we are to honor, respect, and listen to His words. When we hear and trust God, believing that what He says is true, we will be joyful, happy, and blessed! We will also see good results from our hard work.

We all want to know that our lives make a difference in the world. There is no better way to be a blessing to those around us than to trust God and work hard, enjoying the good things God brings from our work.

Day 344

He is the One

Amos 1-3 / Revelation 2:1-17 / Psalm 129 / Proverbs 29:19-20

In your reading of scripture, have you ever noticed some words repeated over and over? In reading Revelation 2, I came across a phrase that I saw repeated three times, but I also realized I had heard this phrase many other times as I've read the Bible. In searching for this phrase in scripture, we will better understand who God is. What is the phrase?

The phrase is "the One who." First, I wanted to confirm who the One is. As we read through Revelation 2:1-17, we discover that the One speaking is Jesus Christ. One clue to His identity is in verse four: "You don't love me or each other as you did at first!"

The first commandment tells us who we must love first:

> "Love the Lord your God with all your
> heart, soul, and strength." —Deuteronomy 6:5.

I hope that one proof is enough to confirm to you that the One is Jesus Christ. In today's reading, we see that He is the One who holds the seven stars in His right hand and who walks among the seven gold lampstands. He is the One who is the First and the Last, who was dead but is now alive (further proof that we are speaking of Jesus Christ). He is also the One with the sharp two-edged sword in His mouth.

Let's look at other verses that speak about the One and find out more about what He's like!

Matthew 11:10 says,

> "This is the one about whom it is written:
> 'I will send my messenger ahead of you, who
> will prepare your way before you.'"

John the Baptizer is the messenger who was sent ahead, and the One he was sent ahead of was his cousin Jesus who is the Messiah.

1 Thessalonians 5:24 reads, "The one who calls you is faithful, and he will do it." Here we learn that Jesus Christ is faithful, and He will do it (keep you blameless.)

Revelation 1:8 states,

> "'I am the Alpha and the Omega,' says the Lord God,
> 'who is, and who was, and who is to come, the Almighty.'"

(Refer to the NIV). In this verse we discover that Jesus Christ is the Alpha (the First) and the Omega (the Last) and that He is eternal, always existing (was, is, and is to come). And the final verse we will consider today (though there are many more) is Deuteronomy 31:8 in the New King James Version which reads,

> "And the Lord, He is the One who goes before you. He will be with you; He will not leave you nor forsake you; do not fear nor be dismayed."

This verse tells us that He goes before us, is with us, and will not leave us. Because we have this promise we can live without fear. I have a feeling that as you read this entry, many more verses came to your mind. "He is the One who..." fill in the blank. There are so many promises in scripture that we could spend the rest of our days on earth finding and meditating on them.

Day 345

Let Your Light Shine

Amos 4-6 / Revelation 2:18-3:6 / Psalm 130 / Proverbs 29:21-22

As Jesus followers, we have been given everything that our older brother Jesus has. If He possesses it, it is also ours. It may be hard to reconcile that the God of the universe gave us, mere humans, power, authority, grace, and mercy, along with so many things that we could spend a lifetime studying and applying all we've been given.

Not all those who follow Jesus are aware of who they are in Him. I want to offer some proof of the authority we have in Christ from today's reading. Revelation 2:26-28 offers that proof and it's a very sobering and exciting passage of scripture to ponder. From the Passion Translation,

"To everyone who is victorious and continues to do my works to the very end I will give you authority over the nations to shepherd them with a royal scepter. And the rebellious will be shattered as clay pots—even as I also received authority from the presence of my Father. I will give the morning star to the one who experiences victory."

These three verses tell us that as we remain victorious and do His work, He gives us authority over the nations. This is not a harsh authority; notice the words "to shepherd." That wording indicates a heart to gather, protect, and teach. One that guides those who gather into truth. Did you also notice that we receive a gift from Jesus Christ? Yes! We receive the morning star, which is Jesus Christ Himself.

Not only have we received Him as Savior and Lord, but we will receive all of who He is. One day we will know Him as He knows us because we will see Him face to face (1 Corinthians 13:12.) What does it mean to call Jesus the Morning Star?

The stars were created to give light, as were the sun and moon. However, these lesser lights were created by the Greater Light, the One who is light. By His very presence, He gives light wherever He is. When we are given Jesus, the Morning Star, we are given the light of truth and love. All that we do will be illuminated by Jesus Christ.

There is a great need for this light in the world today.

Jesus said in John 9:5,

"As long as I am in the world,
I am the light of the world." (English Standard Version)

Imagine how dark this world would be without the light of Jesus in it. His light exists in the world through the church, the followers of Christ. We are needed and we must shine His light brightly.

One of the works that He expects of us is to shine His light into the earth around us. We must not hide who we are and whose we are; to do so would be to condemn the world to sin and death. Because the Father loves humanity, He wishes that no one would die apart from knowing Him. We are the "light shiners." We are the truth bringers. We are love spreaders.

Go. Be light, truth, and love to this dark, confused, and sorrowful world.

Day 346

Jesus is the One Who...

Amos 7-9 / Revelation 3:7-22 / Psalm 131 / Proverbs 29:23

Some Christians get a little bogged down when reading the book of Revelation. There are many reasons for this. One of them is that no one is quite sure what events recorded in this book have already happened and what is in the future. Then there are the differences in whether the Church is taken from the earth before, during, or after the great tribulation this book speaks of. We are not going to talk about any of the controversial topics today.

Instead, I want to speak about the intent of the book of Revelation, what John is revealing. Then I want to reveal someone to you. This is a continuation of an entry I wrote a couple of days ago.

Revelation 1:1-2 in the Berean Study Bible says this,

"This is the revelation of Jesus Christ, which God gave Him to show His servants what must soon come to pass. He made it known by sending His angel to His servant John, who testifies to everything he saw. This is the word of God and the testimony of Jesus Christ."

If we read these two verses properly, John wrote this book based on the revelation Jesus Christ Himself gave to John and asked John to write down. First and foremost, the book of Revelation is intended to reveal to us Jesus Christ. With that in mind, I was interested to find that part of that revelation is hidden in each address made by the Spirit to the seven churches. Here is the list of what I found that describes Jesus Christ.

Among the messages to the seven churches, we see this phrase, "From the One who..." Now that we are aware that "the One" is referring to Jesus Christ, I was excited to learn more about Him. I was also excited to confirm that based on the description, several Old Testament prophets had seen Jesus in visions. Of course, John also saw Jesus Christ as he prepared to write this book.

The messages to the churches are found in Revelation chapters two and three. I have included other scripture references in parenthesis for additional confirmation that these statements refer to Jesus Christ.

> Regarding Ephesus: "This is the message from the One who holds the seven stars in His right hand. The One who walks among the seven gold lampstands." (Revelation 1:20).

> Regarding Smyrna: "This is the message from the One who is the First and the Last (Revelation 22:13), who was dead but is now alive." (Luke 24).

> Regarding Pergamum: "This is the message from the One with the sharp two-edged sword." (Revelation 19:15).

> Regarding Thyatira: "This is the message from the Son of God, whose eyes are like flames of fire, whose feet are like polished bronze." (Daniel 10:6)

> Regarding Sardis: "This is the message from the One who has the sevenfold Spirit of God and the seven stars. (Isaiah 11:2, Revelation 1:20).

Regarding Philadelphia: "This is the message from the One who is holy and true, (Hebrews 7:26, John 14:6) the One who has the key of David. (Isaiah 22:22) What He opens, no one can close; and what He closes, no one can open."

Regarding Laodicea: "This is the message from the One who is the Amen (2 Corinthians 1:20) – the faithful and true witness, (Revelation 1:5) the beginning of God's new creation." (Colossians 1:15-18).

I encourage you to read through the additional verses I've cited because with what we've read from Revelation and what you'll read in the extra reading, you will know much more about the power, authority, and beauty of Jesus Christ. I believe one could study nothing except the One who was and is and is to come for an entire year and still scratch only the surface!

Day 347

The Lord is King!

Obadiah / Revelation 4 / Psalm 132 / Proverbs 29:24-25

As I read the scriptures for today, one phrase stuck out to me and caused so much joy! There are times when we are all reading along, and our brain checks out. We may catch some details and miss others. There are times when we must re-read that last sentence or paragraph because we were not focused enough. But this phrase woke my heart up quickly.

The phrase was from Obadiah verse 21 (yes, it's a one-chapter book of the Bible). The last statement in the verse is,

"And the LORD himself will be king!"

You know, there are times when this world is going crazy with no end in sight. All of us are waiting for the craziness to end and for someone to step in and rescue us. There is nothing that wakes one's heart up more than knowing a Savior has arrived!

When Jesus arrived on earth the first time, he was a helpless infant who depended on his mom and dad for everything — for his very survival. When He comes the second time (and He *is* coming,) He will come as the Sovereign Ruler that He is.

Every eye will see Him.
Every knee will bow, and
every tongue will confess
that He is Lord. (Philippians 2:10-11)

Those knees and those tongues will bow and confess whether they previously believed in Him or not. That's a sobering thought.

Whenever I think about that day of His second arrival on earth, I can't help but imagine what it will look like; what it will be like. I believe it will be both terrifying and exciting. I believe there will be loud noises of worship and praise, and that we will see things we have only imagined. He's arriving with His heavenly army; those sights and sounds alone will be a shock to our humanity.

However, as we see Him, we will be changed. Our new heavenly bodies will better be able to comprehend what we will see and hear. For the first time since we were sent to earth and were born, we will be in the realm from which we came. I wonder if we will remember and feel at home? I believe we will!

Our King will have arrived. Our Rescuer, our Savior will have revealed Himself. The day that we've longed for will have come and gone, then the judgment. The separation of the goats on the left and the sheep on the right will be complete. Are you ready to see Him?

Day 348

Don't be Afraid to Speak

Jonah 1-4 / Revelation 5 / Psalm 133 / Proverbs 29:26-27

When I've read the story of Jonah, I have considered him to be kind of a wimp. Jonah was sent to tell the Assyrians, a very violent and evil people group, that God was going to destroy them. Instead of Jonah obeying God, he got on a ship going in the opposite direction.

Why did Jonah run? Maybe Jonah was afraid of facing the Assyrians with the message of destruction, and afraid they might kill him. However, according to Jonah 4:1-3 it appears Jonah was afraid of something else.

"This change of plans greatly upset Jonah, and he became very angry. So, he complained to the Lord about it: 'Didn't I say before I left home that you would do this, Lord? That is why I ran away to Tarshish! I knew that you are a merciful and compassionate God, slow to get angry and filled with unfailing love. You are eager to turn back from destroying people. Just kill me now, Lord! I'd rather be dead than alive if what I predicted will not happen.'"

When God asked Jonah to deliver this message, Jonah evidently suspected that God would not destroy the Assyrians after they were warned, but that He would instead forgive them if they repented. The verses say that Jonah knew that God was merciful and compassionate. It appears as if Jonah wanted to be a prophet whose warning of judgment would come to pass, not a prophet who turned the hearts of the unrighteous toward God.

Jonah was angry that God wasn't going to follow through and destroy the Assyrians but not because he cared about what happened to them. It was because Jonah wanted his words to come to pass. He was more concerned with his reputation than with the saving of a nation.

When God asks us to speak certain words, do we question Him? Or do we agree to speak based on His word, or based on a certain expected outcome? How hard is it for us to simply obey what God is asking, leaving the results to Him?

God wants us to be His mouthpieces on the earth. Doing so will sometimes cost us our reputation. Either people won't believe what we say, or they will reject us personally, or the outcome we expected won't come to pass and we'll be embarrassed. It can be a lonely life to walk out the calling God placed within us.

Another scripture comes to mind when considering this topic of obeying God by speaking His words. When Peter was imprisoned for preaching about Jesus, upon his release he was warned not to speak in Jesus' Name again.

This was Peter's response in Acts 5:29:

"But Peter and the apostles replied,
'We must obey God rather than any human authority.'"

Peter didn't simply face rejection; he had been put into prison for speaking the truth about Jesus Christ. Most of us will never face prison for speaking about our faith. Yet, we shrink back in fear. Let's not be afraid of the rejection and judgment of men, rather let's be concerned that they must hear God's words, so they can receive truth and eternal life.

Day 349

Let Your Gifts Shine

Micah 1-4 / Revelation 6 / Psalm 134 / Proverbs 30:1-4

Sometimes we are led to believe that unless we're the best at something among those in our circle of family and friends we ought to stay quiet on a topic. I'm not sure why we look for and tend to value only the one who is at the top of their skilled field. We idolize musicians, doctors, philosophers, or any other intelligent or gifted person who has received higher education.

It is not wrong to honor those who have worked hard and achieved great things. However, we must also value each person for the gift of God placed within them. And who is it that determines when someone is the best and the only one to whom we should listen or go to for advice? I believe we can learn valuable information from any person, from the smallest child to the most educated and seemingly wise among us.

When reading Proverbs 30:1-4, I had to do some research to find out who the author was. I had not heard of Agur, the son of Jakeh. After my research, I don't know much more than before I began. But what little I was able to discover led me to speak the way I am. Agur is not mentioned anywhere else in scripture, although it is believed he was alive during the time of Solomon.

One commentary said that he was probably considered to be one of the other wise men of the time when Solomon reigned. I don't know if I'm the only one, but as we read stories, we sometimes forget that the hero of the story is not the only one who... fill in the blank.

Solomon was not the only wise man and not the only leader of his day. He was the most respected and well-known, but there were others.

So, it's interesting that Agur's sayings were included in the scripture in the thirtieth chapter of Proverbs. He made it to the big leagues! There must have been something of importance in Agur's teachings that he would be included in the canon of the Bible. We see from his writings that he was a humble man, not filled with arrogance.

Proverbs 30:3 says:

> "I have not mastered human wisdom,
> nor do I know the Holy One."

After this humble introduction of his skills, Agur goes on for thirty-three verses to share his wisdom which begins in verse four with a description of God's power over the universe. He asks the reader these questions:

> "Who but God goes up to heaven and comes back down? Who holds the wind in his fists? Who wraps up the oceans in his cloak? Who has created the whole wide world? What is His name – and His Son's name? Tell me if you know!"

It sounds to me as if God has been revealing himself to this lesser-known wise man named Agur. And that Agur used his skills as a writer to record his revelations. Let Agur's story inspire you to use the skills you have.

Write if you're a writer. Sing if you're a singer. Speak if you're a speaker. Care for people if you're a physician. Use your hands if you're a craftsman. Use your mind if you're a philosopher.

This list could go on endlessly. Whatever your gifts, be faithful to use them even if you do not consider yourself to be at the top of your field. The talents and gifts you have will be a valuable blessing to someone!

Day 350

Put on the Lord Jesus

Micah 5-7 / Revelation 7 / Psalm 135 / Proverbs 30:5-6

Something interesting has been happening lately when I pray for people. I don't always see this but many times lately I have seen some of them in the Spirit and caught glimpses of their armor. I've seen helmets, breastplates, shoes (which include the shin guards), and I've seen crowns. God has even shown me what I look like in the Spirit, and it was much more impressive than I realized!

When studying about the armor of God from Ephesians 6:10-18, I'm fully aware that not only do we have spiritual armor, but Jesus Christ is our armor. So, while I'm seeing armor in the Spirit, Jesus Himself also guards, protects, and defends each of us. Let me prove that to you beginning with Proverbs 30:5b,

> "He is a shield to all
> who come to Him for protection."

Let's backtrack just a bit and list the pieces of our armor, then we'll prove that Jesus Christ is each piece. Here is the list of our armor from Ephesians 6: the belt of truth, the body armor of God's righteousness, the shoes of peace which are the Good News of the Gospel, the shield of faith, the helmet of salvation, and the sword of the Spirit which is the Word of God.

We've mentioned one proof that the Lord Jesus is our shield of faith from Proverbs 30. Let's find Him in scripture as the belt of truth.

John 14:6, in TPT says,

"Jesus explained, 'I am the Way, I am the Truth, and I am the Life. No one comes next to the Father except through union with me. To know me is to know my Father too.'"

Let's prove that the Lord is our breastplate or body armor of righteousness. The NIV translates 1 Corinthians 1:30 this way, "It is because of him that you are in Christ Jesus, who has become for us wisdom from God—that is, our righteousness, holiness, and redemption."

The Lord Jesus is our Good News shoes. The Gospel is referred to as the Good News. The Gospel is simply laid out in 1 Corinthians 15:1-4 and because Jesus's coming, death, burial and resurrection are central to the Gospel, He is our Gospel of Peace.

The Lord Jesus is our helmet of salvation. Psalm 118:14: "The Lord is my strength and my defense; he has become my salvation." (NIV).

The Lord Jesus is our sword of the Spirit which is the Word of God. To prove this one let's go to John 1:1-4, also reading from the NIV. Here we learn about the Word, "In the beginning was the Word, and the Word was with God, and the Word was God. He was with God in the beginning. Through him all things were made; without him nothing was made that has been made. In him was life, and that life was the light of all mankind."

"The Word" as defined in The Strong's Concordance from John 1, states:

"In John, denotes the essential Word of God, Jesus Christ, the personal wisdom and power in union with God, his minister in creation and government of the universe, the cause of all the world's life both physical and ethical, which for the procurement of man's salvation put on human nature in the person of Jesus the Messiah, the second person in the Godhead, and shone forth conspicuously from His words and deeds."

So, when you are using the Word of God as your weapon (the only weapon you possess), you are wielding Jesus Christ Himself and He is a powerful weapon! I hope you are as convinced as I am that Jesus Christ is our armor.

Now, go put on the Lord Jesus Christ (Romans 13:14) and defeat the enemy!

Day 351

Our Inheritance

Nahum 1-3 / Revelation 8 / Psalm 136 / Proverbs 30:7-9

What is an inheritance? From an earthly perspective, our inheritance consists of the assets and possessions of an ancestor that are passed along to us once that ancestor leaves earth. An earthly inheritance does not last because it is only in our possession while we're on earth.

The inheritance I'm more interested in is the one God gives us spiritually. Yes, He does provide us with physical resources such as food, clothing, shelter, money, etc. But He has also given us an inheritance that will last forever. Our spiritual inheritance exists in the realm of the Spirit but we can see evidence of it in the natural realm.

We'll talk about some of what we've inherited through Christ in a minute, but first I want to show you a verse from today's reading. Psalm 136:21 says,

> "God gave the land of these kings as an inheritance
> – His faithful love endures forever."

This scripture is referring to two kings of the land of Canaan, the land God gave to His people. God took the land away from these evil kings and gave it to His people. They did have to fight for the land, pushing out the evil people who lived there. However, because of God's promise, the land belonged to them in the Spirit before they ever engaged in the first physical battle.

We need to remember this also. God has already given us our

inheritance in the Spirit realm; it is substance, and it is already available. We must accept who we are in Christ and align our hearts and minds with the truth of Heaven before we will see our inheritance manifested in the earth.

Part of our inheritance is heaven, and eternity in the presence of our Lord and Savior.

1 Peter 1:4 says,

"And we have a priceless inheritance—an inheritance that is kept in heaven for you, pure and undefiled, beyond the reach of change and decay."

While no one can fully describe all that waits for us in heaven, Jesus Christ will be our primary focus once we arrive. Revelation 21:4-7 tells us to expect:

"'He will wipe every tear from their eyes, and there will be no more death or sorrow or crying or pain. All these things are gone forever.' And the one sitting on the throne said, 'Look, I am making everything new!' And then he said to me, 'Write this down, for what I tell you is trustworthy and true.' And he also said, 'It is finished! I am the Alpha and the Omega—the Beginning and the End. To all who are thirsty I will give freely from the springs of the water of life. All who are victorious will inherit all these blessings, and I will be their God, and they will be my children.'"

We have inherited eternal life with the ability to see God face to face. We have inherited separation from tears, death, sorrow, crying and pain. We have inherited water to drink from the springs of the water of life. We have inherited many blessings, because we are His children.

Because we belong to the Father through Jesus Christ, all these things already exist for us in heaven. One day we will see, touch, hear, smell, and taste all the good things God has blessed us with. For now, we dream of being with Him forever. We are His and He is ours.

Day 352

The Lord is Our Army

Habakkuk 1-3 / Revelation 9 / Psalm 137 / Proverbs 30:10

All of today's reading was heavy. I read everything from destruction and captivity of God's people in Habakkuk to angels blowing trumpets and releasing plagues on the earth in a time to come. Whew! It is days like this that I am looking for that ray of Holy Spirit to come shining through, and I did find it!

I do not know if you have ever read the book Hind's Feet on High Places by Hannah Hurnard, but it is a story that follows a young woman on her journey from her fearful place of existence to a full, mature relationship with her Savior and Shepherd. I have not read the whole book yet – too many books and too little time! But I would certainly love to finish the story at some point.

However, at the end of Habakkuk 3, I found my encouraging verse and it reminded me of the story of Much Afraid (the young woman in the book mentioned). Habakkuk 3:19 tells us this,

> "The Sovereign LORD is my strength!
> He makes me as surefooted as a deer,
> able to tread upon the heights."

I talked several weeks ago about the word "surefooted" because God had spoken that word about me through a friend. I love that this promise is for all of us, and I pray you will see yourself as the surefooted deer today. Let's look more deeply at this verse to see what nuggets we can gain.

The LORD God is our strength, meaning He is our "strength,

might, efficiency, wealth, and our army." I just love that last definition that says He is our army. It makes me think of the much-used phrase from the 1950s: "You and what army?" A person from that era would use the phrase in response to a threat when they were not willing to back down. If we were aware that the Lord God is our army, we would never back down!

"He makes me as surefooted as a deer, able to tread upon the heights." It is interesting that when looking at the definitions for "heights," or "high places" as read in the King James Version of the Bible; we find that one of the words used is "battlefields." Other meanings for the heights are, "ridge, mountain, and high places of worship." I cannot help but conclude from these two thoughts that the Lord is our army, and he makes us surefooted on the battlefield.

Perhaps one would find other scenarios, or Holy Spirit would offer other encouragement when reading this verse, but today, this is what I hear Holy Spirit saying to us: "We cannot lose with the Lord as our army. We cannot falter on the battlefield with Him by our side." So, do not be afraid of the battle when it comes into your path; the Lord is with you, and He will make you strong!

Day 353

God's Good Reputation

Zephaniah 1-3 / Revelation 10 / Psalm 138 / Proverbs 30:11-14

Have you ever listened to or done business with someone simply because of their reputation or because someone recommended them? Most of us prefer to have experience with someone's good reputation or work before we commit to a long-term relationship with them, whether in business or personal.

If my good friend recommends someone to me, I'm excited to connect with that person because I trust my good friend. If my good friend tells me to steer away from a certain person or company, I do it based on their recommendation. My husband is a contractor in our area and since May of 2000, he has worked hard to build a good name in the community. He's a small contracting company but he has the reputation of having integrity and doing excellent work.

As we talked before, there is power in the meaning of a person's name. Our names have spiritual significance based on their origin and meaning. But there is also an aspect of having a good name based on how we've presented ourselves to the world. All of us would prefer that when our names are spoken, someone hearing the name will think well of us.

There is a verse in today's devotional reading that grabbed my attention, Psalm 138:2. It says,

"I bow before Your holy Temple as I worship. I praise Your name for Your unfailing love and faithfulness; for Your promises are backed by all the honor of Your name."

Has anyone ever promised you something but then did not deliver on that promise? Or has anyone promised you something, then did exactly what they said they would and more? It's the second one we can be assured of when considering the promises God has given. If He has said it, He intends to follow through and make it happen all for the sake of His Name.

If we read something in the Bible, or if we truly hear God speak, we can hold on to what we've read or heard and be certain of it coming to pass. Sometimes when we hear God speak, we imagine the answer before it happens. It would be better if we left the imagining up to God because what He has planned for us is always better than we can envision.

1 Corinthians 2:9 TPT says,

"Things never discovered or heard of before,
things beyond our ability to imagine –
these are the many things God has in store
for all His lovers."

This verse is what convinces me that I would rather ask, seek, and knock, and then leave the answering up to God. What He wants to do for and in me will always be much greater than I can understand.

We trust God first because of His great Name. His reputation is secured by his Name that is above all other names. His Name declares His good character. As we learn the way He does things, we come to trust Him further based on His consistent character and works.

Day 354

A Brave Prayer

Haggai 1-2 / Revelation 11 / Psalm 139 / Proverbs 30:15-16

God wants to have such a deep friendship with us that we allow Him to reveal to us the deepest, hidden places of our hearts. Because God sees and knows all things, He is fully aware of our motives and hidden sins. However, since God loves us fiercely, His knowledge of our imperfections is balanced with His love. Because we are His, He will never destroy us when He finds wrong motives within us.

Instead of scolding us to maturity, He chooses to love and forgive us in our growth. He knows that we will be drawn by His kindness and love, therefore, He always leads with love. His people are lavished with love while his enemies are left with His anger and disapproval.

Psalm 139 is an intimate look at the relationship between God and us: between the Creator and His creation. There is an invitation in the last two verses that we will focus on today.

Psalm 139:23-24 says,

"Search me, O God, and know my heart; test me and know my anxious thoughts. Point out anything in me that offends you and lead me along the path of everlasting life."

How many of us are brave enough to pray that prayer? Maybe we are brave on the surface, but when it comes to sitting in our secret place with our heavenly Father, we may suddenly find ourselves to be shy. If we truly take the time to consider the words in these two verses, we may hesitate to make them into a prayer.

May I suggest we start small? What if we began with just the first phrase: "Search me, O God, and know my heart." Then allow Him to search and know. Since He already knows, this will be more a revelation for you than for Him. Don't be surprised if you hear Him tell you a few things He sees.

He won't tell you to condemn you or make you feel bad. He will show you what He shows you because He sees how it hurts you. And when something hurts you, that causes Him great pain. For those of you who have children, you know how difficult it is to see them suffer.

When our children are feeling lonely, sad, angry, frustrated, or hurt, or when they are sick and there's nothing we can do to make them feel better, we get a glimpse into how our heavenly Father feels when we are suffering. I promise He feels the same (and greater) affection for you than you do for your children.

After you have allowed Him to search you, and to tell you a few of the things He finds, consider continuing the prayer one phrase at a time. It may take you several days to work through these two verses. There is nothing wrong with taking plenty of time to pray through these verses. Especially when we consider we are growing massively in doing so.

Once you've made it to the end of these two verses, you'll be reminded that your reward is eternal life. Eternal life is yours through Jesus Christ, not because you got all the answers correct on the test! Eternal life is yours because you are His and He loves you!

Day 355

God to the Rescue!

Zechariah 1 / Revelation 12 / Psalm 140 / Proverbs 30:17

I don't know about you, but I enjoy the conversations the writers in Psalms have with the Lord. They are real and raw, holding nothing back. Whether the writer is frustrated, angry, sad, fearful, joyful, or thankful, the reader is not left guessing about their mood. Some might be afraid to speak so honestly with God in prayer, but I happen to believe He prefers honest speech.

Sometimes I chuckle when the psalmist is complaining about the wicked and asking God to destroy them. How many times have we wished we had someone who would beat up the bully for us? It's as if the psalmist is calling on his dad or older brother to protect him when he's being cornered and threatened.

There are times we all feel that way. We feel taken advantage of, abused, neglected, and bullied. Most of the time we must sit quietly and take it for fear of starting a fight where someone will get hurt. However, when considering a spiritual fight, we don't ever need to feel we must be quiet. God is always prepared to defend us.

Psalm 140:9 is an example of wishing our enemies would get what's coming to them:

"Let my enemies be destroyed
by the very evil they have planned for me."

That might seem wrong to say, but since everyone reaps what they sow, inevitably, those who plot and plan evil will eventually fall right into their own trap.

The Psalm ends as it should with the writer seeing God for who He is and with a thankful heart for having been heard. The writer also knows that God will win in the end. Let's look at verses 12-13,

"But I know the LORD will help those they persecute; He will give justice to the poor. Surely righteous people are praising Your name; the godly will live in Your presence."

Even when we're afraid and complaining, we must conclude that God is good, and He is protecting us from those who are evil. Yes, we may suffer things but ultimately, we will be saved and will be with God for all eternity. Nothing can take that gift away from us!

Day 356

The Beauty of Wonder

Zechariah 2-3 / Revelation 13 / Psalm 141 / Proverbs 30:18-20

As we get near the end of the year and the end of our reading, there are some serious and intense scenes in the texts. All the minor prophets, from Hosea through Malachi, as well as the book of Revelation, are filled with difficult-to-understand events and imagery. I'm not even going to attempt to explain the book of Revelation.

Yes, there have been parts that stuck out to me, ones I have brought to you in devotional form. When Holy Spirit highlights something, that's what I choose to bring to you. Today, I am interested in looking further at two verses from Proverbs 30. Verses 18 and 19 have a few topics that could take more time than we have. Let me include those two verses here, then we'll talk about them.

"There are three things that amaze me – no, four things that I don't understand; how an eagle glides through the sky, how a snake slithers on a rock, how a ship navigates the ocean, how a man loves a woman."

These are things that amaze Agur – remember our little-known writer mentioned a few days ago? They are not things he's willing to explain, but only to mention. That brings me to conclude that we don't need to know and understand everything. That's saying a lot for someone who loves to know why and how things work!

But I also love a good mystery, and I certainly love surprises. Sometimes we must accept the things God has created around us for what they are without trying to take the mystery out of them. It's okay and good for us to be left wondering. We will never fully grasp the deep mysteries surrounding God or the way He does things. So, I believe it's perfectly okay to allow these four things mentioned to be left in that space of awe in our hearts.

If we understood all things, there would be no need for faith and trust. That would also mean there would be no need for God because we would be self-sufficient. To settle upon ourselves as sufficient is to settle for less than what God has for us. His sufficiency is far greater than our own. And it is fully available to us.

So, read those two verses again, and as you do; allow your mind to picture that eagle gliding through the sky, that snake slithering across the rock, the ship sailing strongly through the ocean, and the smile of love.

Allow yourself to wonder and to dream, to hope and to believe. After all, we are in the season of hopes and dreams and new beginnings. Be blessed today!

Day 357

Don't Eat the Worm!

Zechariah 4-5 / Revelation 14 / Psalm 142 / Proverbs 30:21-23

I'm sure you've each had moments or seasons where you felt overlooked and unloved. People are busy, they have their own lives to live, and their own drama to walk through. So, others don't always have time when something dramatic or difficult happens. When that happens to you, and it will, you have two options when responding.

We can respond with understanding by realizing those who appear to be absent are likely overwhelmed by their own situations. Or we can pout, sulk, and complain, "Nobody likes me, everybody hates me. I think I'll go eat worms!" That last bit was for a little humor on our potentially sour attitude. Now that I've quoted those funny words, I'll have to share their origin.

These words are the beginning of a Thirteenth-century rhyme that originated in Tonga. I'm not going to quote the rest here because reading them makes me queasy! If you'd like to read the rest, feel free to do an internet search for the words above and the whole thing will pop right up.

While we're feeling sorry for ourselves, I believe we've forgotten that there is One who is always aware, listening, and caring about what is happening to us. Psalm 142:4-5 tells a short story about the complainer suddenly realizing he is being heard.

"I look for someone to come and help me, but no one gives me a passing thought! No one will help me; no one cares a bit what happens to me. Then I pray to you, O Lord. I say, 'You are my place of refuge. You are all I really want in life.'"

It may sometimes take us a while to realize that we're looking in the wrong place for affirmation and a listening ear. Hopefully, as we mature in our relationship with Jesus, those times of complaint become shorter, and we more quickly realize God hears our every word. Not only does He hear, but He also has the answer to each situation and question.

So, the next time you're tempted to go out into the garden to eat worms; as you pick up the shovel to dig, say a little prayer. I have a feeling you'll put the shovel down, laugh at the silliness and begin to feel as if you really do matter to someone. While you're feeling that way, remember to spend time thanking Him for hearing and loving you!

Day 358

A New Law

Zechariah 6-7 / Revelation 15 / Psalm 143 / Proverbs 30:24-28

As a worship leader, I always have a song playing in my soul; sometimes several songs are playing one after the other. Today I have a song in my soul and another that I've read from scripture. As I listened to both, I found a beautiful correlation. I'll begin by sharing the song from Revelation 15, then I'll share a verse from the song in my heart.

Revelation 15:3-4 says,

"And they were singing the song of Moses, the servant of God, and the song of the Lamb: 'Great and marvelous are your works, O Lord God, the Almighty. Just and true are your ways, O King of the nations. Who will not fear you, Lord, and glorify your name? For you alone are holy. All nations will come and worship before you, for your righteous deeds have been revealed.'"

Now the verse, then I'll share my thoughts. This is from "O Holy Night", that beautiful Christmas song. "Truly He taught us to love one another; His law is Love and His gospel is Peace; Chains shall he break, for the slave is our brother, And in His name all oppression shall cease, Sweet hymns of joy in grateful chorus raise we; Let all within us praise His holy name!"

Whenever we sing this song, I can feel everyone's hearts soaring at the amazing majesty of our God being revealed by Holy Spirit. The parts that tie together in the "Song of Moses" and the "Song of the Lamb" from Revelation 15 and the verse from "O Holy Night" are these:

> "They were singing the song of Moses
> and the song of the Lamb. And His law is Love
> and His gospel is Peace."

In the Old Covenant, followers of God were subjected to offering sacrifices of grain, oil, wine, and animals so they could be right with God; that is the song of Moses, the law. But when the Lamb came to earth, lived a sinless life, died, was buried, and rose again, a new law was enacted, the Law of Love. We no longer must offer sacrifices for ourselves because Jesus Christ offered Himself in perfection and has removed our sin.

That's why I especially enjoy the words from "O Holy Night" that confirm His law is Love. We are no longer held prisoner by the law that brought death; we have been graciously brought into a New Covenant through no work of our own. We were brought in because we are loved.

As we read through the rest of verses 3 and 4 in Revelation 15, we are struck with the power, majesty, strength, and glory of God, to whom we belong. It's difficult to grasp the fullness of what we've been given in Christ. As we wait tonight to remember His coming, embrace the beauty of His Law of Love that is being poured out on you and yours!

Day 359

Prince of Peace, Enter in

Zechariah 8 / Revelation 16 / Psalm 144 / Proverbs 30:29-31

Although I read through all the scriptures for today, because it is near Christmas Day, I have a song on my heart. As I was singing the song, I decided to look up the lyrics and I was struck with what a powerful truth this song tells. There are times when the old hymns and poems are best, and I think this is one of those times.

"I Heard the Bells on Christmas Day" began as a poem written on Christmas Day in 1863 by Henry W. Longfellow. It was later put to music in 1872 by John B. Calkin. Here are all the powerful words for you to enjoy:

> "I heard the bells on Christmas day.
> Their old familiar carols play,
>
> In music sweet the tones repeat,
> 'There's peace on earth, good-will to men!'
>
> I thought how, as the day had come,
> The belfries of all Christendom
>
> Had rolled along Th' unbroken song
> Of peace on earth, good-will to men!
>
> And in despair I bowed my head.
> 'There is no peace on earth,' I said.
>
> 'For hate is strong - And mocks the song
> of peace on earth, good-will to men!'

Then pealed the bells more loud and deep:
'God is not dead, nor does He sleep!

For Christ is here. His Spirit near
brings peace on earth, Good-will to men.'

When men repent and turn from sin
The Prince of Peace then enters in.

And grace imparts within their hearts
His peace on earth, good-will to men.

O souls amid earth's busy strife,
The Word of God is light and life.

Oh, hear His voice, make Him your choice,
Hail peace on earth, good-will to men.

Then happy, singing on your way,
Your world will change from night to day.

Your heart will feel the message real.
Of peace on earth, good-will to men."

Merry Christmas to you and yours! May God richly bless you as you gather to celebrate His first coming.

Day 360

Create a Legacy

Zechariah 9 / Revelation 17 / Psalm 145 / Proverbs 30:32

We've talked before about how I taught all my children at home. I didn't do it because I thought it was a good idea; I did it because when Matthew was 2 years old, God told me to teach them at home. I didn't know anything about homeschooling, but God quickly connected us with others who were on the same journey. This was in a time before homeschooling was as popular as it is today.

I have three grown children and all three were taught at home from birth to high school graduation. All three are successful in their chosen fields. One is a gifted musician and computer techy type, the next one took general education courses for nursing before heading toward being a horse trainer and a mom, and is completing her certification as an integrative nutritionist, and the last one has one degree and is working in the corporate world while working to further her education to be prepared to climb the corporate ladder.

I'm proud of them all. The thing I'm most proud of is that they chose their paths. I saw their skills and gifts early on and worked hard to give them the basics of good character, Bible training, and a solid education. Then it was up to them to hear God and choose a vocational path.

The part of their schooling that I found to be most valuable, was that we read the Bible daily. That way, they heard God's Word as small children and still hear it in many ways today. There is a beautiful mandate in Psalm 145:4 that affirms God's word to me about homeschooling.

"Let each generation tell its children
of Your mighty acts; let them proclaim Your power."

You don't have to homeschool your children to tell them about God's mighty acts and His power, but it certainly was handy to have them as a captive audience every day. It is very important that we properly convey God's greatness, power, authority, majesty, beauty, love... and many other things to the next generation. This is because knowing God as He truly is supplies each generation the needed anchor to survive as the world gets crazier!

Give your children and grandchildren hope by diligently revealing Jesus Christ to them. Give them what you have, then study to learn so you can give them more. Feed yourself first, then feed those littles. In doing so, you will create a beautiful legacy!

Day 361

Servant Leaders

Zechariah 10-11 / Revelation 18 / Psalm 146 / Proverbs 30:33

If you have ever been under the direction of poor or abusive leadership, you will appreciate what's on my heart to share today. I will not speak derogatorily of leaders, but I hope to shed some light on the topic. If you have served under a caring servant-leader, you are blessed indeed!

To begin, let's look at Zechariah 10:2-3 to see what God did when there was bad leadership among His people:

"Household gods give worthless advice, fortune-tellers predict only lies, and interpreters of dreams pronounce falsehoods that give no comfort. So, my people are wandering like lost sheep; they are attacked because they have no shepherd. 'My anger burns against your shepherds, and I will punish these leaders.' For the Lord of Heaven's Armies has arrived to look after Judah, his flock. He will make them strong and glorious, like a proud warhorse in battle."

First, perhaps the reason God's people were turning to idols, fortune-tellers and dream interpreters is because the priests who were called to shepherd or pastor them were failing at their job. The leadership was corrupt; they lead the people away from God and into idolatry. As a result of poor leadership and looking in the wrong places for answers, God's people were confused and lost.

God was not angry with the people for their confusion; He was angry with their shepherds, or as we would call them, their pastors. How does a pastor get so far off track? I believe one way is by him neglecting his own personal relationship with God. A true servant-leader spends time with his heavenly Father first, then feeds the people with what he's been given. That way everyone's needs are met.

A servant-leader cares for others above his own reputation and desires. He (or she) listens to God and works hard to build up and encourage those under his care. He looks closely at those God brings, finds their special gifts, and looks for ways to cultivate those gifts, so the people have a strong sense of fulfillment in the Kingdom and so that God receives maximum glory.

The servant-leader must also take care of his own spiritual needs. However, sometimes he may serve to his own detriment for the good of others. Leadership is not glamorous; it is a life of hard work and self-sacrifice. Leadership is not always fun, but it is fulfilling if you are serving in the capacity God has called you.

If you find yourself under poor or abusive leadership, seek the advice and counsel of God and of other leaders outside the situation. You need to hear the Lord for yourself as well as through those other trusted leaders so that you will know how you should respond in such a situation. Sometimes you will be asked to stay while God makes shifts in the current leadership. Sometimes God will move you out.

No matter what God speaks, rest assured you will be cared for! God loves you more than any man or woman is able. He will step in and correct a situation in one way or another. It's beautiful that the Lord of Heaven's armies stepped in to look after Judah, His flock. He will do the same for you, so do not fear.

Day 362

Until Jesus Returns

Zechariah 12-13 / Revelation 19 / Psalm 147 / Proverbs 31:1-7

There are times when I'm reading my Bible and my heart soars, tears come to my eyes and there's a huge lump in my throat. The scene being described can overwhelm me with expectation and joy, especially at the thought of seeing Jesus face-to-face. I came upon a portion of scripture today that did just that. It had my insides jumping up and down.

Revelation 19:11-16 says,

"Then I saw heaven opened, and a white horse was standing there. Its rider was named Faithful and True, for he judges fairly and wages a righteous war. His eyes were like flames of fire, and on his head were many crowns. A name was written on him that no one understood except himself. He wore a robe dipped in blood, and his title was the Word of God. The armies of heaven, dressed in the finest of pure white linen, followed him on white horses. From his mouth came a sharp sword to strike down the nations. He will rule them with an iron rod. He will release the fierce wrath of God, the Almighty, like juice flowing from a winepress. On his robe at his thigh was written this title: King of all kings and Lord of all lords."

I'm so excited reading and imagining this scene that I can't stand it! With that first sentence in verse eleven, I thought of the scene from the Lord of the Rings movie, The Two Towers when Gandalf comes over the hill on a white horse just as the sun is rising. Up until that point, King Theoden and his army were being overrun as they attempted to defend Helm's Deep. But when Gandalf appeared, the battle turned.

And when the One who is Faithful and True, the one who is the Word of God, the One who is King of all kings and Lord of all lords returns, our battles will be done! Can you imagine that day! Imagining His return gives us hope to continue to stand, fight, and believe.

We cannot allow ourselves to give up when we become tired in the fight. Yes, we will get tired, frustrated, confused, and even lonely at times. However, that is when we need to remember there is a big picture within the story of our lives. We are here for such a short time, then the next generation will come, then the next. Then when the time is right, Jesus will appear and take His people to live with Him.

Galatians 6:7-9 in TPT is helpful when considering how to live daily.

"God will never be mocked! For what you plant will always be the very thing you harvest. The harvest you reap reveals the seed that you planted. If you plant the corrupt seeds of self-life into this natural realm, you can expect a harvest of corruption. If you plant the good seeds of Spirit-life you will reap beautiful fruits that grow from the everlasting life of the Spirit. And don't allow yourselves to be weary in planting good seeds, for the season of reaping the wonderful harvest you've planted is coming!"

So, while we wait for His return, let's plant good seeds of life in the Spirit. While we're planting, let's not allow ourselves to become discouraged or tired because if we continue to be faithful, a blessing will follow. Go grab your gloves and your shovel and get to work!

Day 363

Be Brave, Speak Up

Zechariah 14 / Revelation 20 / Psalm 148 / Proverbs 31:8-9

Have any of you been bullied? Or were you ever a bully? Bullies behave as they do for various reasons. Sometimes it's because they are afraid. Or because they are being bullied by someone else and becoming a bully helps them feel powerful. Whatever the reason, at the heart that bully is afraid.

I've heard stories of others who befriended the mean person and soon discovered that they were softer on the inside than they first realized. When I was in high school, I had one bully try to mess with me. It was kind of ridiculous. There was a boy who liked me. We were talking and she decided she wanted him. So, she threatened to fight me for him. I laughed and told her she could have him. I was not getting into a fistfight over a boy! Plus, if he couldn't stand up for himself or me, I didn't want him anyway.

Then there was the time we were visiting friends in South Carolina. My sister and I were small, maybe eight and ten. I was inside with one friend cutting up a snack of celery, while my sister and another friend were outside. When the girl cut the celery, a piece fell on the floor. She said we would give that to my sister since she didn't know. I secretly hated that idea, so when we got outside, I told my sister what had happened. Don't mess with my sister!

These two scenarios are mild, and no one was under any threat, however, there are times when someone's life is in danger, and we must decide how we're going to respond. I understand we want to be careful not to endanger our own lives to rescue another. Sometimes it's enough to tell the right person who has the authority or power to help.

Proverbs 31:8-9 says,

> "Speak up for those who cannot speak for themselves;
> ensure justice for those being crushed.
> Yes, speak up for the poor and helpless,
> and see that they get justice."

We must not remain silent when we see injustice. There are hidden (and not so hidden) evils in the world today and we need to find a way to stand for truth in the face of evil. Standing always includes prayer, but sometimes it includes more.

It may include giving our resources and/or time. It may involve phone calls or emails. Whatever it is that you believe God wants you to do to respond when someone is being victimized, be bold and act. God and heaven will back you up.

You'll also find that you're not alone. Many stand and speak for the truth. Don't be fearful. You may just save someone's life.

Day 364

Singing in the Bed

Malachi 1-2 / Revelation 21 / Psalm 149 / Proverbs 31:10-24

It's confession time. I am not a lover of early mornings; I never have been. Yes, I had to be up by 6:00 in the morning to catch the bus to school, but if given the choice, I'd sleep until about 8:00 after having gone to bed around midnight. Some are early birds, and some are night owls. I wonder why both sayings involve birds...

Those who love mornings enjoy teasing those who don't and vice versa. How many of you have heard, "I don't see how you lay around in bed all day!"? Well, I personally don't see how you are so chipper and happy in the morning. My brain takes a few hours to gain full function even after my feet hit the floor. Today's verse touches on my humorous side as you'll see.

Psalm 149:5 says,

> "Let the faithful rejoice that He honors them.
> Let them sing for joy as they lie on their beds."

See? I can stay in bed and still sing! That sounds very promising to me. I haven't tried to lay down during a time of corporate worship; I'm sure that would be frowned upon.

When I was pregnant with Abigail and on bedrest, we used to take a lounge chair and place it off to the side in the sanctuary so I could still attend church. Hm, come to think of it, I have worshiped from my bed, uh lounger... If it is first the heart that sings, I believe we can worship God anywhere. That is the point of this verse.

We must not save our worship only for corporate gatherings where others will see us. We must also make time to worship and pray when we're alone with God. Each expression will look different, depending on whether we have a band, a radio, or only our voice. But if our hearts are worshiping, God is pleased and blessed.

So, just for kicks, the next time you're lying on your bed, try a little worship. Your spouse may think you've lost it, but that's ok. Jeff is usually asleep so my worship will have to be quiet. I usually pray in a whisper as I'm settling down. I suppose I can also sing in a whisper.

Day 365

We Will See His Face

Malachi 3-4 / Revelation 22 / Psalm 150 / Proverbs 31:25-31

Let's first acknowledge that this entry is the final one for the year. This devotional compilation was originally written in the year of our Lord 2021, but whenever you read it, you will find relevance for your walk with Jesus Christ. That is because the Word of the Lord stands firm forever. (1 Peter 1:25)

God's Word will always be beneficial to your life and will bring answers to the questions you have. You may not find specific answers, but you will find a principle that aligns with God's love and justice.

As I finished reading the Bible today, I was struck with the majesty, strength, and beauty that was being described in each entry. Malachi spoke of the day of judgment. Revelation spoke of the coming of the Lord and what we will experience in heaven as God's beloved people. Psalm 150 was filled with praise and noisy celebration. And Proverbs praised the value of a godly woman.

With a full heart, I must say the thing I most look forward to is seeing Jesus Christ face to face. Revelation 22:4 says,

"And they will see His face,
and His name will be written on their foreheads."

Isn't that why we are faithfully following God's Words? Isn't that why we hopefully worship Him? There is a culmination coming, whether in our lifetime or after we've moved to heaven. At some point, we will see and touch our Reward.

As I've stated several times over the past year, our Reward is a Person. Truth is a Person. Our Armor is a Person. None of the things we have read were received in a vacuum; they are all tangible and real. Some read the Bible as if it were a fairy tale, or as if it is history in the long distant past, as though the people involved couldn't have been real.

The people were real, our God is real, the facts as they were recorded are real and our hope for the future and eternity with Father God is real. The things we've read and studied are more than concepts on a page. The things we've read about are the things that have been and that we will one day experience.

So, as we close out this year and as we look with expectation toward the next year, let's remember the words we've taken into our souls. Let's allow Holy Spirit to cause these words to come alive and to refresh, build and encourage us. And, as you've been refreshed, look for ways to be a blessing and refreshment to others God brings into your path.

I wish you a beautiful, strong, and prosperous new year. May you see Him in ways you never have, and may you experience all He has planned for you. Commit to tithe your time to Him this year, not just your money. There are twenty-four hours in a day. How might you set aside time just for Him? I'm going into the new year with a renewed commitment to sit at His feet and listen. Will you join me?

Biography

Maria Kear began her Jesus journey when she received Christ at the age of five. That dramatic encounter with Him set her up for a life filled with a spiritual hunger that compels her to not only seek after God wholeheartedly, but also to create hunger and thirst in others through her words, experience and life example.

Maria and her husband Jeff have three adult children and as of this writing they have four grandchildren with more promised in the future.

Maria and Jeff launched a house church called Bethesda Springs House of Mercy and Grace in July 2020 when the Lord surprised them with His plans as they fasted and prayed just prior.

Maria has many fond sayings, one of which is, "I want to leave this earth with my hair still on fire!"

May your "hair" catch fire as you read and become hungrier for Him.

www.ingramcontent.com/pod-product-compliance
Lightning Source LLC
Chambersburg PA
CBHW021706120626
46545CB00004B/1431